THE HEALTHY ANOINTED LIFE

Walk in YOUR Healing, in Every Area of Your Life!

By Earlene L. Dotson, Ph.D./ Health Science

Editor/Contributor: Dionne Felix, Ph.D.
Copy edited by: Devie Phipps
Interior formatting/design: Morris Dotson

www.xulonpress.com

The Healthy Anointed Life
115 Penn Warren Dr.
Ste. 300-178
Brentwood, TN 37027

DEDICATION

This book is dedicated to my Lord and Savior Jesus Christ who inspired and enabled me to write about our incredible journey towards my total restoration. Thank you for loving me with an everlasting love.

To my husband Morris and to my children: Lena, Kibwe, Lorna, and Ryan, for their support and encouragement in the writing of this book. May this book aid you in your walk towards wholeness and total restoration in every area of your life.

To mom Lucy (86 yrs. young) and mom Edith (87 yrs. young) for such awesome, healthy (ageless) genes. Mom Lucy has more energy and gets around better than most—half her age.

To Dr. Amanda Berry for putting the fire under me to finish this book. Thank you for your friendship and I hope that this book will inspire you and motivate you to finish your own book which tells the story of how the Lord is leading you towards health and wellness.

Finally, I want to dedicate this book to my sister Delores, for teaching me how **not** to ever give up or give in, no matter how tough it gets. You have pressed through many years of pain and suffering, but God has baffled all the doctors and has brought you through. Every year is a testimony of how God can sustain and strengthen us through our crisis!

ACKNOWLEDGEMENTS

There are many family members and friends who were supportive throughout this process. I would like to acknowledge them for their love, support, and prayers during my recent illness. Without their untiring prayers and faith, I would not be as well as I am today and this book would not have been written.

To my husband, Morris, for coming through for me at the last moment and working long hours to make sure this book was properly formatted and looked professional. You are truly a keeper!

I would like to especially acknowledge Dionne for lending her editorial gifts and contributing valuable insights and feedback in the book. I want to also acknowledge Devie for looking over the manuscript and putting the finishing touches on the final draft. You are greatly appreciated.

Thank you Darnyce, for the many talks (tears), prayers, and visits that you made to Tennessee to check on me and encourage me to keep the faith. You are truly loved. Special thanks to my brothers George and James (JD) for collaborating with me and encouraging me regarding the writing of this book. I am looking forward to reading your book that is soon to be published.

Thank you Lavern for being there during the lowest points of my life. You are always so positive. You are truly like a sister to me. We have been through some things together that many will never understand. Aren't you glad that it is God's desire to heal and restore us? I pray and praise God everyday for you. I would like to acknowledge Brenda R. and Melissa B. for coming through just at those moments when I was tempted to give up or give in.

Thank you (alphabetically) Annette, Annick, Barbara, Betty (Boop), Charlotte, Deborah, Dekota, Devie, Don and Lynette, Edie, Gina, Larraine, Shirley and Robert, and many others, for encouraging me throughout this awesome project. You guys are the best!

CONTENTS

Introduction

Psalm 30:2-3 – O LORD my God, I cried out to You, and You healed me. O LORD, You brought my soul up from the grave; you have kept me alive, that I should not go down to the pit.

This book is a result of the inspiration of what God has done for me in healing me of a grave and incurable (based on the doctor's view) disease. The promise is true; I cried out to God (The Great Physician) and He has healed me—not just physically, but also mentally, spiritually, emotionally, socially, and occupationally. My faith journey has taught me that it is God's desire to heal each one of us; however, we must be willing to be healed His way and not our way. Also, Jesus has taught me that He is able to heal us in every area of our lives; so no matter what aspect of healing you are in need of, God is able to help you experience "the healthy anointed life."

"God declares the end from the beginning and from ancient times things that are not yet done" **(Isa. 46:10)**. Do you know what this means? It means that God has declared your healing even before you were yet healed. He has already declared your victory over every habitual sin even before you experienced the victory. From the onset of your disease, physical limitation, addiction or emotional drama, God already declared your healing. If He spoke it, He will bring it to pass and if He purposed it, He will do it **(vs. 11)**. There is no need to fear; God has already declared it (your healing) from the beginning. *"Do not fear, nor be afraid; have I not told you from that time, and declared it? You are My witnesses. Is there a God besides Me? Indeed there is no other Rock; I know not one"* **(Isa. 44:8)**. Jesus asks us "if there is a God besides Him." The answer is emphatic; "Indeed there is no other Rock; I know not one!" Believe and be healed! As believers of the living God, we are admonished "to walk by faith and not by sight" **(2 Cor. 5:7)**. We must not base our faith on what we see, feel or touch; our reality is the Word of God. Take God at His Word and walk in your healing in every dimension of your life.

Holistic Health

When Jim Fixx, a famous runner, suddenly died in 1984 at the age of 52, many were stunned and bewildered. Some people considered Fixx the epitome of fitness. In other words, he was a fitness guru. But as his history began to unfold, it became apparent that Fixx had been a chubby 220-pound, 2-pack-a-day smoker, and a junk food addict during his mid thirties. However, he began to turn his life around by including exercise in his daily program, replacing the sedentary lifestyle he previously enjoyed. He not only began exercising, but he also became a world-class runner who helped to add to the fitness and running epidemic in the 70s. How could a man, who had run approximately 70 miles per week for at least 12 years suddenly, die of a heart attack while running one day? Perhaps a holistic approach to health might have made a difference. A holistic wellness lifestyle requires an integrated approach to well-being. "It is not enough to be a fitness superstar or a health food junkie—you need to experience wellness in every dimension of health. Wellness is a holistic state of being known as "healthy living."[1] This holistic approach promotes the interrelationship and unity of the body, mind, and spirit.

1 Thessalonians 5:23 *Now may the God of peace Himself sanctify you completely; and may your whole spirit, soul, and body be preserved blameless at the coming of our Lord Jesus Christ.*

The scripture verifies that God requires a complete consecration of the mind, body, and soul. This suggests that human beings are holistic creatures comprised of various dimensions of health and well-being. Health, in the Biblical setting, refers to wholeness and wellness. Wellness, sometimes used interchangeably with health, is specifically defined as a state of optimal health that includes the physical, mental (intellectual), spiritual, emotional, social (environmental), and occupational.[2] Environmental wellness is closely associated with social wellness; social wellness relates to a person's social environment and community interaction. Each of these dimensions of health is interrelated and emphasizes the essential sphere of human existence, which creates harmony and balance, and characterizes the "whole person." The "whole person" in terms of its various dimensions of health, can be defined in the following explanations.

The physical dimension emphasizes a persons' ability to carry out daily tasks without fatigue. It includes physical fitness in terms of cardiovascular endurance, muscular strength and endurance, flexibility, and body composition. It encourages proper nutrition as well as practicing other healthy lifestyle behaviors, while discouraging the abuse of drugs, tobacco and alcohol. The physical elements of health also include our personal responsibility in relationship to routine medical check-ups, screenings, and safety precautions. According to Sackney,[3] "If the body is kept strong, fit, and well nourished, it will be able to resist illness."

The intellectual (or mental) element of health centers on one's ability to learn, be creative, and to use knowledge and skills effectively. The intellectual dimension encourages the discovery and development of personal gifts to be shared with others.[4] According to Myers,[5] the intellectual domain includes problem solving and creativity and "is necessary for healthy brain functioning and hence quality of life across the life span. It is a holistic aspect involving the ability to develop new or different concepts, ideas, structures, or products. Creativity is increased in individuals who possess high confidence in themselves and has a positive effect on life satisfaction, and overall wellness."

The spiritual dimension of health centers on a person's belief, purpose, and meaning of life. It recognizes the belief in God and emphasizes one's morals, ethics, and values. Although the spiritual component often appears obscure to some, it is the most important part of the biblical and secular holistic model of wellness. There are several studies that support the positive outcomes of spirituality on recovery from addiction, substance abuse, [6,7] teen sexual activity, [8] depression[9] and other programs.[10] Additional support for the validity and importance of the spiritual aspect of health was established by Myers and Williard, [11] who stated that since the 1990s, there has been an increased awareness of the importance of religion and spiritually on our national life.

The emotional dimension highlights a person's ability to manage stress, convey emotions, and accept limitations. Numerous people are unable to experience or display happiness, passion or affection, as well as other human emotions. As a result, the quality and quantity of relationship events within their lives are hampered.[12] The emotional domain encourages maintenance of satisfying relationships as well as the ability to live and work independently, while realizing the importance of seeking and appreciating the support and assistance of others.[13] Research suggests that negative emotions such as anger, hostility, and stress are associated with an increased risk of hypertension, coronary artery disease, and even death.

The social dimension focuses on an individual's environment and community. It involves the development and maintenance of relationships with others as well as respecting and being tolerant of the opinions and beliefs of others. Additionally, the social aspects of health encourage promotion and preservation of our world by encouraging health measures to enhance the quality of life.[14] "Social health involves the quality of our relationships, satisfaction in our social roles, our sense of belonging and feelings of love and acceptance."[15] Ideally, social health is cultivated throughout the early stages of life and childhood, within the confines of a loving family environment. This nurturing process propagates psychological benefits of enhanced self-esteem and self-worth.[15]

The occupational dimension accentuates personal satisfaction and enrichment in one's life through work. Essentially, it encourages the ability to balance work and leisure as well as the development of a person's beliefs and attitudes toward work or his or her occupation. The choice of employment, job satisfaction, career endeavors, and personal performance are all components of occupational health.[16] A person's life work serves as the ability to support him or her, as well as others, for maintenance of life. Work is also directly related to feelings of competence, life satisfaction, and self-confidence.

I want to re-emphasize the fact that each of these dimensions of health interrelates with each other and can have a positive or negative influence on our overall well-being. In order to help you completely understand this unification concept, I have addressed each dimension in chapters 4-9.

The Anointing

Deuteronomy 7:6 — *For you are a holy and set-apart people to the Lord your God; the Lord your God has chosen you to be a special people to Himself out of all the peoples on the face of the earth.* **(Amplified)**

2 Corinthians 1:21 — *But it is God Who confirms and makes us steadfast and establishes us with you in Christ, and has consecrated and anointed us.* **(Amplified)**

1 John 2:20 — *But you have an anointing from the Holy One, and you know all things.*

1 John 2:27 — *But the anointing which you have received from Him abides in you, and you do not need that anyone teach you; but as the same anointing teaches you concerning all things, and is true, and is not a lie, and just as it has taught you, you will abide in Him.*

The term "anointed" has different meanings for different people. The word *anointed*, in relationship to this book, refers to a consecrated person or being. This anointing from Christ abides in us and guides us in every aspect of our lives *(1 Jn. 2:27)*. Biblically speaking, the word *anointed* comes from the Hebrew word *mashiyach* (maw-shee-akn). The noun *mashiyach* really means messiah; however *mashiyach* as a verb implies the anointing "for a special office or function" (Strong's Expanded Dictionary). As a point of interest, the act of anointing a person with oil in the Bible was a sign of consecration and/or was used as a remedy to heal the sin-sick soul (see **Mk. 6:13; Lk. 10:33-34; Jas. 5:14; Rev. 3:18**). God told Jeremiah (**1:5**) that before he was formed in his mother's womb He knew him, and before he was born He consecrated and appointed him to be a prophet. Likewise, God has set each of us apart or consecrated us for His Divine purpose. In every area of our lives we should glorify Him who anointed us for a special work. "The Healthy Anointed Life," can be summarized as a life consecrated to God in every dimension of health (physical, spiritual, mental, emotional, social and occupational), and is a life that is governed by God's ways of healthy living and not man's version of how to be healthy, wealthy, and wise.

As you read through this book, there will be instances where I encourage you to pause and reflect on the ideas I present. In these instances, I simply ask you to **"pause and reflect"** and carefully consider what you have read, before you continue on. May you be blessed as you ponder the various points of reflection.

Chapter I

Holistic Healthy Beginnings

> **Romans 8:29** — *For those whom He foreknew, He also destined from the beginning to be molded into the image of His Son that He might become the firstborn among many brethren.*
> **(Amplified)**

Physical

God ordained man, from the beginning of time, to be healthy and vibrant. A perfect pair created in the very image of God. They were placed in the Garden of Eden to represent God's perfect handiwork and to bear the image of God both in their outward appearance and in integrity and character. He established Adam and Eve in a holistic healthy environment. Their physical needs were perfectly fulfilled. The food was delicious and nutritious with no additives, preservatives, pesticides, genetically modified organisms (GMO), monosodium glutamate (MSG), or artificial flavors! Fruits, grains, and nuts (**Gen. 1:29**), in their natural state, comprised their very simple diet. The only "soft drink" or beverage they drank to quench their thirst was pure water from the rivers that flowed through the Garden of Eden (**Gen. 2:10**; **Rev. 22:1**). Their home was surrounded by indescribable beauty. The four riverheads, the blue skies above, the unfading flowers of every hue, various trees with their diverse foliage and fruit, lovely vines, and green grass, embodied their lovely home. The air was clean, clear, and healthy. The climate was always perfect so there was no need for covering; besides, the radiance of God's presence covered them with the light of His glory.[1]

Emotional and Social

This paradise, in which the first couple lived, would have been futile in producing absolute happiness if they did not have the companionship and love of each other. God knew that Adam needed Eve to complete him and to share love with someone like himself. I can imagine God performing the first wedding ceremony on earth. I don't know that it was very elaborate (no bridesmaids, groomsmen, best man or maid of honor), but to have the Creator of the Universe sanction and bless the first marriage is an awesome thought! Marriage was a blessing then and it can be a blessing now if we would abide by the

Divine principles God has ordained for husband and wife. Adam and Eve's union not only fulfilled their emotional and social needs, but it elevated their physical, mental, and spiritual composition. They were equal partners sharing the blessings and benefits of their delightful environment. Just think for a moment what it would be like for man and woman to perfectly relate to each other **(*Pause and Reflect.*)** Because of their social needs, God created them (male and female) to commune with the angels and the creatures of the earth for companionship and fellowship.[2]

Spiritual

Have you ever thought about how fantastic it will be to talk face to face or walk hand in hand with Jesus? It was the privilege of the Edenic couple to walk and talk with Jesus in the garden during the evening (**Gen. 3:8**). How excited and joyful they must have been in anticipation of their time they would spend with God. Our spiritual nature can only flourish and strengthen as we walk and talk with Jesus, everyday, through the power of the Holy Spirit. How much time do we spend in communication with the living God (see chart in Chapter 8)? Are we anxious and joyful at the thought of meeting with God in the morning and evening? **(*Pause and Reflect.*)**

Occupational and Intellectual

Another blessing that God endowed the first dwellers on earth was that of occupation. They labored each working day in the garden "to dress it and keep it" (**Gen. 2:15**) looking good. God appointed man his occupation as a blessing, to engage his mind, strengthen his body, and develop his inherent potential. Intellectually speaking, "the Garden of Eden was the school-room, nature was the lesson book, the Creator Himself was their Instructor and the parents of the human family were the students."[3]

As the crowning act of the healthy living principles established in the beginning, God anointed (consecrated) the seventh-day Sabbath as a day of rest for man (**Gen. 2:2-3**). This special day was specifically set apart for Adam and Eve to reflect upon their Creator's handiwork and to commune with their Maker. How important is it for us to give God one day out of seven to reflect upon His goodness, setting aside all of our worldly interests and concerns? (***Pause and Reflect.***) The Sabbath day was set aside for us to worship Him who gives us "every good and perfect gift," and to fellowship with fellow believers.

There are crucial lessons that we can learn from our first parents in relationship to "the healthy anointed life." It is the Lord's desire for us to enjoy health through the simple and natural means that He provides. Perhaps, if possible, we need to get away or move to a more country-like environment, where we can breathe in the fresh air and bathe in the sunlight. We should eat foods in its simplest form—without all of the grease, salt, and sugar. Drink pure water instead of soda or other sugary drinks, coffee, tea, etc. Get away from the Internet and TV (video) for a while and plan some outdoor activities. From time to time, change your environment during your time with God and worship and praise Him in an outdoor setting (park, etc.), which is more conducive to hearing and talking with Him. I am fortunate to live in a house that has a covered deck overlooking hills and wooded grassy areas. Some of my greatest aspirations and inspiration have engrossed my thoughts as I sit out on the deck, witnessing God's wonderful nature.

From the beginning, it has been our Designer's master plan for us to be anointed (consecrated, set apart for a special purpose) in all dimensions of our being. The Bible says, "I beseech you therefore, brethren, by the mercies of God, that you present your bodies (*physical, mental (intellectual), spiritual, emotional, social (environmental), and occupational*) a living sacrifice, holy, acceptable to God, which is your reasonable service (***Rom. 12:1***)."

Chapter II

Holistic Health
Depredation of Sin

> **Genesis 3:22, 23** — *And the Lord God said, Behold, the man is become as one of us, to know good and evil; and now, lest he put forth his hand, and take also of the tree of life, and eat, and live for ever; Therefore the Lord God sent him forth from the garden of Eden, to till the ground from whence he was taken.*

One of the saddest commentaries regarding the fall of our first parents is found in **Gen. 3:1-23**. Adam and Eve disobeyed God and Satan was given the authority to rob them of all of their earthly authority and health-sustaining life. The word *depredation* means to rob or plunder. Sin robbed the Eden dwellers in every dimension of health.

Intellectual Depredation

Adam and Eve bought into the lie of Satan that the fruit from the tree of good and evil was more desirable than the fruit from the other trees, and that it would make them wise. There are many today who are being robbed of health and vitality because they believe Satan's lie in relationship to appetite and worldly wisdom. Sometimes, we are convinced that we know what's best for us and that God's ways are insignificant, outdated, and cannot be scientifically substantiated. We eat what God tells us not to and we are suffering the negative consequences of sickness, disease, and premature death. God has given us counsel in His Word on every aspect of our lives, but we refuse to follow His ownership manual and the results are sickness, divorce, crime, discord, strife, and death (both physical and spiritual).

Spiritual Depredation

The first thing that Satan robbed Adam and Eve of was the radiance of God's presence, which was the light of His glory that covered them. They immediately sensed that they were naked and began to sew fig leaves together to shield themselves from their nakedness, which was really an awareness of guilt because of sin. They hid from the same God they looked forward to meeting with joy and great anticipation prior to their fall. Sin always condemns and separates us from God. When questioned by God regarding their whereabouts, they began to make excuses for why they were hiding from Him. Then, when God asked them if they had eaten the fruit from the tree that He had explicitly told them not to partake of, they began playing the "blame game." Adam blamed Eve and Eve blamed the serpent, but neither "fessed up" to the role they played in sinning against God.

The blame game has continued throughout the history of the world, even to the present. We are still making excuses for why we break God's law (moral, physical, health, etc.). We blame other people for provoking, enticing, pressuring, and convincing us to do wrong. We even blame God for creating us with our emotions, passions, appetite, and inherent needs.

Emotional Depredation

Second, Satan robbed our first parents of peace and harmony that existed when they were equal partners. Now Adam was to take the sole position of being the head of the family and he would rule over Eve. Eve thought that by partaking of the forbidden fruit she would be elevated in her position, which was at her husband's side, but she fell beneath it. Since then, there has been a fierce battle of the sexes: men demanding their headship and women refusing to submit.

Occupational Depredation

Satan also robbed Adam and Eve of a life of carefree living and pleasant occupation. Their vibrancy began to diminish and work became hard. Cursed was the ground and in the sweat of man's brow they were to eat bread, which now included the herb of the field. As noted in the first chapter, man's original diet consisted of fruits, grains, and nuts but, after sin, vegetables were added to man's diet (**Gen. 3:18**). It has often been said that fruit cleanses the body and vegetables heals the various systems of the body. It is a known fact that vegetables contain more phytochemicals than fruits, which protects against disease, especially cancer. Perhaps God, in His wisdom, added vegetables to aid in healing the body in its depraved state. (**Pause and Reflect.**) The ground was cursed with thorns and thistles; in fact, all creation was cursed because of sin. A life of toil and care became man's fate and mortality became our destiny. Adam and Eve did not die immediately; they did eventually, and death would be the lot of every man and woman.

Physical and Social Depredation

Adam and Eve were asked to leave their home of paradise and live on the earth where the curse of sin was already present. The very atmosphere on earth had been tainted by sin, which meant that the temperature changes would vary greatly. The Lord, in His mercy, provided them with clothes to shield them from inharmonious changes of the earth's environment. I can imagine the sadness of our first parents when they began to witness death and decay all around them. The flowers would bloom, fade, and then die. The leaves on the trees would fall because of decay, and the animals began to prey on each other. Although the Bible does not specifically state that God sacrificed an animal or two for the purpose of clothing the human pair, it stands to reason that He did. Imagine the horror of our first parents as they witnessed, for the first time, death. The same animals that they petted, caressed, and lovingly played with, they now see lifeless and cold.

Chapter III

Healthy Holistic Restoration through Christ

Jeremiah 30:17 — I will restore your health and heal your wounds, says the Lord...

I have heard it said that in the gift of Jesus Christ all heaven was poured out on our behalf. You may ask, "What does that mean?" It means that by the sacrifice of our Lord Jesus Christ, all have been redeemed from the curse of sin, and everything we lost can be restored. It means that through Christ all things are possible (*Phil. 4:13*) and that includes the restoration of the mind, body, and soul. Christ came to restore and heal everything that Satan had stolen from us. He came to renew our health physically, spiritually, intellectually (mentally), emotionally, socially, and occupationally (*Isa. 53:5*). *Psalm 23:3* says that "He restoreth my soul ..." To restore means to re-create, renew, or bring back. God wants to bring us back to the holistic healthy state that He ordained from the beginning; however, in order to avail ourselves of Christ's holistic healing, we must get to know Him on a personal level (*Jn. 10:1-15*). In *John 10:4*, Christ says that His sheep know Him and obey His voice (Word). Do you know how to recognize His voice (Word) from all other voices that may be calling? (*Pause and Reflect.*) Believe it or not, God is more anxious for us to hear His voice and get to know Him, on a personal level, than we are. I like how the **Amplified** Version of scripture puts it, "And therefore the Lord waits (expecting, looking, longing) to be gracious to you; and therefore He lifts Himself up that He may have mercy on you and show loving-kindness to you. For the Lord is a God of justice. Blessed are all those who wait for Him, who expect and look and long for Him" (*Isa. 30:18*).

After sin robbed humanity of our prosperity through health, Jesus stepped in to restore what we had lost. An example of God's willingness to restore is found in the Biblical account of the deliverance of the Israelites from slavery in Egypt. Jesus wanted so badly to be with His people that He instructed Moses to build a sanctuary so that He could dwell with them (*Ex. 25:8, 22*). God initiated the restoration process by providing a worship center where the children of Israel could be brought near to Him and worship Him, the True and Living God. God is anxious to dwell in the hearts of His dear children and His presence is always in the midst of those who assemble together to "worship Him in spirit and truth (*Jn.*

4:24). The sanctuary that the Israelites built was symbolic of Jesus Christ who would later physically dwell with men (***Jn. 1:14***).

The God of the Universe had big plans for the children of Israel. They were to prosper in every sphere of wellness. They were to possess holiness of character that reflected more and more the character of God (***Deut. 4:39, 40***). This is where we are to begin to allow God to initiate the restoration process. Without holiness of character it is impossible to move to the other aspects of restoration. In addition to holiness of character they were to be, without rival, the most physically healthiest specimens on the face of the earth (***Ex. 15:26; Deut. 7:13-15***). Sickness, disease, and infirmities were to vanish completely if they heeded to the health principles laid out by their Master. They were to be the most intelligent—not lacking in wisdom, understanding, discernment or soundness of mind. Their land was to be restored to the beauty and fertility present in the Garden of Eden. They were to be the most skillful in their various trades and careers and unparalleled in prosperity and wealth. In summary, it was God's intended purpose for them to be the greatest nation in the world. Unfortunately, because they refused to obey God's holistic health principles, they failed in reaching the "healthy anointed life" that God ordained for them to possess.

The good news is that God has the same desires and plans for spiritual Israel (us) that He had for Israel of old and that is to prosper us in every area where they failed. You see, the devil deceives us into thinking that we can be perfectly healthy without obeying God's laws. We must remember that Satan is "the father of lies" and he comes to us only to steal, kill, and destroy but Jesus came to give, impart life, and restore (health and healing).

Psalm 23:5 also emphasizes the anointing; "....thou anointest my head with oil, my cup runneth over." David was anointed with the physical and spiritual oil of gladness because of the plenteous blessings given him from the Lord. When the Holy Spirit anoints us, we are overwhelmed with His sanctifying influences and all the blessings that come our way as sons and daughters of the almighty God. God wants to anoint us with spiritual oil, symbolizing a life consecrated to Him in every area (dimension) of our life.

Matthew 17:11 *Jesus answered and said to them, Indeed, Elijah is coming first and will restore all things.*

The healthy anointed life is a life of restoration, healing, and re-creation. Give your broken-down and fractured life to the One who can heal and restore every aspect of your life. Jesus died that we may have life—life more abundantly (**Jn. 10:10**). It is by His stripes that we have been healed (**1 Pet. 2:24**).

Chapter IV

The Physical Anointed Life

> **3 John 2** — *Beloved, I pray that you may prosper in all things and be in health, just as your soul prospers.*

Although the above verse differentiates between the prosperity of the physical body and the prosperity of the spiritual man, it is evident that John's desire is that we prosper mentally, physically, and spiritually (in every way). God is not just concerned with our spiritual well-being; He is also concerned with our physical and temporal needs. In fact, God created human beings holistically in nature, and every dimension of man is intimately intertwined. Most Christians believe that they can neglect the physical areas of their lives because they are doing good works for God; however, they fail to recognize that God is a God of balance, and the physical laws of health that He has ordained are essential to the availability of

His blessings and restorative powers. In **Exodus 15:26**, God says *"if you listen, listen obediently to how God tells you to live in his presence, obeying his commandments and keeping all his laws, then I won't strike you with all the diseases that I inflicted on the Egyptians; I am God your healer"* (**Message**).

During my illness, the above promise became adamantly clear. I was diagnosed with an incurable disease, and the doctors told me that the best they could do was to wait to see how the disease would progress and then give me chemotherapy treatments until I die. They could not cure my disease; my only hope was to receive chemotherapy to hopefully prolong my life. This was indeed devastating news! At first I wept—you know, that kind of weeping that just swells from the pit of your stomach—and I questioned God's rationale. *Why God? Why would you allow me to experience this grave illness, especially when I had tried to live a healthy lifestyle?* I cried and prayed, and prayed and cried. As my disease continued to progress, I began to experience a host of swollen lymph nodes that were pressing against my neck, my throat, and my ear lobes. I prayed earnestly to the Lord and He spoke this promise into my spirit: *"It doesn't matter if you have a hundred swollen lymph nodes, I **AM** the Lord that heals you."* God was beginning to birth in me His plan for my life and how faith, hope, and obedience in His Word were a part of my journey towards physical restoration.

We must carefully listen (through His Word) and do the things that He would have us do in every dimension of our life including the water we drink, the food we eat, the relationships we form, the God we serve and worship, the education we attain, the people we interact with, and the activity we participate in.

God created us to move—to be active. If you have ever broken an arm or a leg and it was in a cast for weeks or months, when the cast was finally removed, that arm or leg became weak because of the lack of movement. Although we know that physically active people live longer and receive many additional benefits, most of us don't exercise. Physical activity and wellness are not a current part of America's way of life. Only 20% of American adults exercise at a moderate intensity level five or more days per week, and only about 14% exercise at a vigorous intensity level for three or more days per week. Physical inactivity and unhealthy lifestyles are the greatest threat to our health and longevity.[1]

The physical anointed life involves a lifestyle that includes physical fitness, proper nutrition, rest, drug-free living as well as the adoption of healthful practices or behaviors that aids in the reduction of risk factors of disease and improves energy levels and well-being.

Physical Fitness

If a pill could significantly lower the risk of heart attack, diabetes, stroke, osteoporosis, cancer, while reducing weight, cholesterol levels, constipation, depression, impotence, increase muscle mass, flatten the belly, reshape the thighs, relieve stress, raise levels of energy, extend longevity, slow down the aging process, and make you better looking—and had no negative side effects—there would be hysteria and frenzy in the streets! The American economy would shift into utter anarchy. The military would have to be called in to secure supplies of this medication. Luckily, there is no such pill; however, there is a way to receive all these benefits and more without a pill. These benefits and more can be obtained by participating in a physical fitness program and a comprehensive wellness program.

What does it mean to be physically fit? It doesn't mean that you have to be able to run a marathon, pump iron, or have definitions in your arms, abs, chest and legs. Believe it or not, you could actually succeed in accomplishing these physical feats but still not be physically fit. Physical fitness refers to the ability to carry out your everyday duties and responsibilities without being so tired that you are worthless for the rest of the day. When people are physically fit, they should be able to walk (jog, cycle, or other aerobic activities) briskly for 2-3 miles, possess muscular strength (lifting, carrying items with relative ease), and maintain flexibility (bend, stretch without pain or discomfort). Physical fitness also requires that you keep the body in proportion, in terms of the amount of body fat versus lean muscle tissue.

Below is a formula for becoming or maintaining physical fitness:

➢ Participate in an aerobic activity(s) for 40-60 minutes 5-6 times a week.
➢ Make sure you are in your training (heart rate) zone. Sweating is a good thing.

> ➤ Engage in some type of weight training exercise regiment, 2-3 times per week.
> ➤ Perform stretching exercises 3-4 times per week.
> ➤ Always start and end your exercise session gradually (warm-up, cool-down).

Wholesome Nutrition

Proper nutrition means that a person's diet is supplying all the essential nutrients to carry out normal tissue growth, repair, and maintenance. Too much or too little of any nutrient can cause serious health problems. The typical diet, of people in America today, is too high in calories, sugar, fat, protein, salt, and not high enough in fiber.

Scientific evidence has long linked good nutrition to overall health and well-being, but what diet does God commend? Can we eat **anything** with prayer and thanksgiving and still be blessed with physical health? (**Pause and Reflect.**) God said that "whatever we eat or drink, we should do to the glory of God (**1 Cor. 10:31**)." Do we glorify God when we eat or drink things that make our bodies sick? The answer, of course, is "no." Believe it or not, the Bible has a lot of counsel on what we should eat and drink.

In the beginning, God gave Adam and Eve fruits, grains, nuts, and later vegetables to eat (**Gen. 1:29; 2:16; 3:18**). I believe this to be the original diet for man. If we would eat these foods in abundance and in their natural state, our bodies would reward us with health, vibrancy and energy. So, you are probably asking, what about meat? As you read your Bible, you'll find out that God gave man permission to eat meat after the flood when most of the plants and trees were destroyed. However, there were some stipulations that were given by God in reference to the type of meat they should eat and how the meat should be prepared.

In **Leviticus chapter 11**, God instructed Moses about the types of food (meat in particular) we should eat or not eat. "The animals that were acceptable for human consumption were those that chewed the cud and had a split hoof" (**v.3**). In terms of the animals of the sea, only creatures with fins and scales were permissible for eating. This mandate was not necessarily just for the Jews, because God made the distinction between clean and unclean foods back in Noah's time (**Gen. 7:2**), before there was a Jew.

Another stipulation was made from God regarding how to eat the clean meats outlined in **Leviticus 11**. In **Genesis 8:4; Leviticus 3:17; 7:23, 26,** God said that the meat should not be consumed with the blood and the fat in it. The blood of the animal must be drained and the fat cut off. Why? Because the blood is the life of the animal. Have you ever gone to McDonald's or Burger King and ordered a burger and asked them to hold the blood and fat? Of course not, you just eat the burger. So, even if we eat the clean meats and don't drain the blood and cut off the fat, we are breaking God's dietary laws (**Ex. 15:26**). I believe that if we would follow the dietary laws given by our Creator, there would be less disease, sickness, and premature death.

Did you know that the average risk of heart disease, for a man eating animal products such as meat, eggs, and dairy, is 50%? The coronary risk for a man who leaves off meat is only 15%. However, the risk of a vegetarian who leaves off meat, eggs, and dairy products is only 4%.[2] According to an editorial in the Journal of the American Medical Association, a total vegetarian diet can prevent up to 90% of our strokes and 97% percent of heart disease. It is a known fact that most of the foods that are high in cholesterol and saturated fats are from the animal kingdom. These foods can become the precursor to hypertension, heart disease, cancer and a host of other unhealthy conditions.[3] Shouldn't the Creator who made us, know what the best food for the body is? *(Pause and Reflect.)*

Based on the deplorable conditions of the animals that we consume,[4] unless you are able to breed you own, I believe it would be best to abstain from eating meat entirely or in limited amounts. As much as possible, try to eat mostly whole grains, fresh fruits, and vegetables. God says of these you may freely eat *(Gen. 2: 16)*. I can personally testify of the tremendous benefits of vegetarianism (chapter 13 – personal testimony).

The basic principle in wholesome nutrition is to choose low fat foods that are unrefined, such as whole grain products, fruits and vegetables. If you eat meat, choose only kosher lean meat. Eat more vegetable protein such as legumes (dry beans), tofu, and low fat meat alternates. Nuts are also very nutritious but should be consumed sparingly (about a hand full per day).

Rest

The average adult in the US sleeps approximately 6 hours or less per 24 hour period; however, research has shown that in order for us to perform at our peak, we need 8-9 hours of sleep per night.[5] There are basically two stages of sleep that we experience during our resting periods: the non-rapid eye movement (NREM), and the rapid eye movement (REM). The most important stage is the REM sleep because it is the deeper phase of sleep. This is the stage where our brain becomes more active in sorting, analyzing and filing new information. It also plays a key role in our learning ability and memorization. Perhaps one reason why we forget many things might be the fact that we are not getting enough rest. **(*Pause and Reflect.*)** The REM stage of sleep recurs approximately every 70 to 90 minutes after we go to sleep. In order for the body to complete the active process described above, we must have four or five active brain periods each night. Towards the morning of the sleep cycle, the NREM stages decrease and the REM sleep increases. If you only sleep six hours or less, your body may feel rested but, in order to be at your best, you may need longer periods of REM sleep.

Job 33:15-16, says that "In a dream, in a vision of the night, when deep sleep falls upon men, while slumbering on their beds, then He opens the ears of men, and seals their instruction." Notice that it is during the deep phase of sleep that God seals our instruction. Perhaps this may be a clue to having God's Word and instructions implanted in our minds. **(*Pause and Reflect.*)**

Disease and Drugs

God has blessed us with clean, flexible arteries at birth, but excessive fat and cholesterol in the diet can clog them. Eventually this chokes off the oxygen supply to vital organs. Most medical treatment, at best, is temporary. If we want to stop heart disease from being the number one killer in North America, lifestyle change seems to be the most logical solution. In North America, every third adult has high blood pressure. This puts them at risk of diabetes, heart attack, stroke, and other debilitating diseases.

The major causes of death in the US are lifestyle-related: 1) Cardiovascular disease and cancer are the first and second leading cause of death; they account for approximately 62% of all deaths in this country; 2) The third leading cause of death is cerebrovascular diseases and, 3) The fourth leading cause of death is chronic lower respiratory disease, which is primarily related to tobacco use.[6]

Based on current figures:

- ➤ Approximately, 9 of 10 causes of death are related to lifestyle and common sense.
- ➤ The "big four" lifestyle related causes of death are tobacco use, poor diet, inactivity, and alcohol. These are responsible for more than 80% of the annual deaths in the United States.
- ➤ Thus the individual controls 80% or more of disease and quality of life.[7]

There is also a link between lifestyle factors and many cancers. Smoking, obesity, consumption of alcohol, and diet that is high in animal products and fat account for 70 - 80% of all cancers. One in five people in North America develop diabetes at some point in his or her life; yet, this disease can be prevented and even cured. Low fat, both in the diet and on the body, and exercise (especially strength training) may be the best cure.

There is a lot of discussion concerning the effects of drinking alcohol, especially wine, in moderation. Is it okay to drink a glass of wine everyday to calm the nerves or for medicinal purposes? Let's first look at some of the scientific evidence concerning the effects of alcohol in moderation and then examine some of the biblical principles regarding wine. When one consumes only 5 ounces of table wine the following occurs:

> ➢ The central nervous system is severely affected (depressant).
> ➢ There is a reduction in inhibitions
> ➢ Dehydration occurs.
> ➢ There is a decrease in fine motor skills.
> ➢ Brain activity is impaired, and
> ➢ Attention, judgment, and control are seriously compromised.

The list of these adverse effects of alcohol consumption increases as one consumes more alcohol.[8]

So why does the Bible approve of drinking wine? Or does it? There are many texts in the Bible that disapprove of drinking wine: 1) **Leviticus 10:8-11** "Do not drink wine or intoxicating drink, you, nor your sons with you, when you go into the tabernacle of meeting, lest you die. It shall be a statue forever throughout your generations, that you may distinguish between holy and unholy and between unclean and clean, and that you may teach the children of Israel all the statutes which the Lord has spoken to them by the hand of Moses;" 2) ***Proverbs 20:1*** "Wine is a mocker, strong drink is a brawler, and whoever is led astray by it is not wise;" 3) ***Proverbs 23:31-33*** "Do not look on the wine when it is red, when it sparkles in the cup, when it swirls around smoothly; at the last it bites like a serpent, and stings like a viper. Your eyes will see strange things, and your heart will utter perverse things," and 4) ***Habakkuk 2:5*** "Indeed, because he transgresses by wine, he is a proud man, and he does not stay at home. Because he enlarges his desire as hell, and he is like death, and cannot be satisfied, he gathers to himself all nations and heaps up for himself all peoples."

There are also many Bible texts that approve of drinking wine, for example, ***Genesis 27:28*** "Therefore may God give you of the dew of heaven, of the fatness of the earth, and plenty of grain and wine," ***Psalm 104:14-15*** "He causes the grass to grow for the cattle, and vegetation for the service of man, that he may bring forth food from the earth, and wine that makes glad the heart of man, oil to make his face shine, and bread which strengthens man's heart," ***Isaiah 55:1*** "Ho! Everyone who thirsts, come to the waters; and you who have no money, come, buy and eat. Yes, come, buy wine and milk without money and without price," and ***Amos 9:13*** "Behold, the days are coming, says the Lord, when the plowman shall overtake the reaper, and the treader of grapes him who sows seed; the mountains shall drip with sweet wine, and all the hills shall flow with it."

You are probably wondering whether or not the Bible is contradicting itself. There are several Hebrew and Greek words for wine in the Bible that may explain the apparent discrepancy. Wine in the Hebrew (yayin) and wine in the Greek (oinos) refer to the juice of the grape either fermented or unfermented throughout the scriptures.[9] In view of the facts presented regarding the harmful effects of even one glass of alcohol, it seems inconceivable that Jesus who produced between 120-180 gallons of wine for the use of men, women and children, would produce wine that had an intoxicating effect. The Bible states in **John 2:10** that after "the guests have well drunk"—referring to the amount of wine that the guests of the wedding feast of Cana had already consumed before Jesus produced the "good wine." There was no indication from the Bible that anyone was drunk even after they had been drinking a lot of wine. Considering the fact that the wine was given to minors, it seems improbable that the drink Jesus produced at the wedding of Cana was anything other than fresh, unfermented, grape juice.

Various research studies have encouraged the use of red wine (fermented) because of its benefits in relationship to heart health among French people. The fact is that the beneficiary properties flaunted in these recent studies are primarily from the antioxidant, resveratrol that is found in dark red and purple grapes. Resveratrol helps to reduce blood clots and low-density lipoprotein (LDL—the not so good cholesterol). The truth is that resveratrol is found in both red wine and grape juice. I believe the better choice of beverage would be pure grape juice or eat red/concord grapes, that way we can benefit from the antioxidants that aid in the reduced risk of heart disease and, at the same time, prevent the adverse effects of just one glass of red wine.[10]

Marijuana is considered the drug of choice primarily with the younger population. There are over two million people in the United States who experiment with this drug every year. Of the two million that use the drug, over a half (1.3 million) are adolescents.[11] What is it about this drug that entices and attracts numerous users, especially the younger generation? I believe that these individuals buy into the lie that it has medicinal properties and that there is no harmful side effects. The fact is marijuana is a dangerous drug that adversely effects and destroys the mind, body, and possibly the soul. The properties of marijuana primarily includes; the mind-altering chemical tetrahydrocannabinol (THC) along with about 400 other chemicals. The majority of these chemicals are carcinogens (agents that cause cancer). Some of the risk factors involved in using this drug includes: impaired judgment and motor coordination, shortened attention span and distractibility, anxiety and panic attacks, depression, problems with memory and learning and an increased risk of schizophrenia.[12] Because marijuana is a psychoactive substance (changes how the brain works), it goes directly against the counsel of God that states that our minds (*"Let this mind be in you which is also in Christ Jesus,* **Phil. 2:5**) and our bodies belong to God (**1 Cor. 6:19**).

There are men and women that are enslaved to marijuana to the point—that all of their means and ambitions are centered on its use. This is just how the devil would have it because there is a definite misplacement from the God who restores the mind, body, and spirit to a god who destroys the mind, body, and spirit. The good news is that God is able to break any destructive habit, addiction or strong hold in our lives (**2 Cor. 10:4-6**).

Chapter V

The Intellectual (Mental) Anointed Life

> **Philippians 2:5** — *Let this mind be in you which was also in Christ Jesus.*
>
> **1 John 2:27** —*But the anointing which you have received from Him abides in you, and you do not need that anyone teach you; but as the same anointing teaches you concerning all things, and is true, and is not a lie, and just as it has taught you, you will abide in Him.*

Having the mind of Christ is the highest form of education that anyone can ever obtain. God ordained from the beginning that the mind be disciplined, educated, and trained for the service of God and man. Regardless of our station in life,

God has entrusted each of us with mental faculties to be developed and used to glorify His name. Therefore, He has given us the ability and responsibility to develop, improve, and cultivate the various gifts, abilities, and talents imparted to us. It is God's plan that we continually acquire knowledge, wisdom and understanding throughout our lifetime.

One of the greatest challenges, in the development of the mind, is self-discipline. Self-discipline comes as a result of training. That's why I believe it is so important to train our children to be disciplined and adhere to the principles of God. When we train our children in the Lord, He will aid them in their study, cultivation, observation, and reflection of their minds. The Bible says to "train up a child in the way he should go, And when he is old he will not depart from it (**Prov. 22:6**).

It is quite difficult to discipline the mind when there are so many distractions and allurements. The "mind is a terrible thing to waste," but unfortunately we waste a lot of time cultivating habits that keep us from reaching the full potential that God's anointing can supply. Too much time is invested in all kinds of amusements, self-gratification of the appetite, schemes for wealth or obsession with fashion. Please don't misunderstand me. We need recreation, and should enjoy the food we eat. We also, should strive for economic freedom and look our very best; however, I am referring to the amount of time and effort invested in these activities to the point of neglect of the development of mind, body, and soul. Our habits of eating, drinking, sleeping, working, worship, etc., must be systematically planned to produce the mental anointed life that reflects the mind of Christ.

Even as I write this book, there are many distractions present to pull me away from completing this chapter—this book. As a University Professor, Chair of the Department of Health, Wellness and Physical Education, I have had the opportunity to teach the course Sports Psychology. One of the cognitive theories emphasized in the course dealt with how athletes need to "gate out competing stimuli" from fans or opponents in order to successfully perform a skill or play. These competing stimuli are distractions from noise, objects rustling in the air, gestures by the opponents or even internal thoughts and pressures. Regardless of what the distractions, the athlete must learn to ignore, tune out or turn a deaf ear to them in order to accurately execute the intended sport or play. In the spiritual field of study, we too must "gate out competing stimuli" in order to develop and execute the intended purpose which God has for us in the procurement of the intellectual anointed life. Every intellectual skill must be practiced. Self-discipline doesn't come overnight; it must be rehearsed and perfected by determination and by the power of the Holy Spirit. Self-discipline "comes in hits and misses, in successes and failures as we try to practice it day after day."[1] The apostle Paul admonishes us to "fight the good fight of faith" (*1 Tim. 6:12*). So don't get discouraged if you organized your very productive day but when the day ended you had not accomplished all that you set out to do. Try it again the next day, and the next, until you have reached the mental anointed, God appointed life goals.

As followers of Christ, we have received the anointing of Christ that abides and instructs us in all things (*1 Jn. 2:27*). It is the Apostle John's desire that the anointing of the Holy Spirit be upon every Christian and totally influence the development of not only the mind but also the body and soul.

Chapter VI

The Spiritual Anointed Life

> *Galatians 5:16 — I say then: Walk in the Spirit, and you shall not fulfill the lust of the flesh. For the flesh lusts against the Spirit and the Spirit against the flesh; and these are contrary to one another, so that you do not do the things that you wish.*
>
> *2 Corinthians 1: 21, 22 — Now He who establishes us with you in Christ and has anointed us is God, who also has sealed us and given us the Spirit in our hearts as a guarantee.*

The spiritual anointed life is a non-carnal life that originates with God and is therefore in harmony with God. The spiritual anointed person is one who walks by the Spirit and manifests the fruit of the Spirit. I can imagine that you are probably thinking that this is an impossibility considering our carnal natures that have been interwoven in the things of this world. You are absolutely correct that in our own flesh we can never obtain the godly characteristics that define the spiritual anointed life; however, it is God who establishes, anoints, and seals us through Christ Jesus. God has given us the Spirit as a guarantee. So through the indwelling of the Holy Spirit we can experience a spiritual transformation that enables us to "walk in the Spirit."

What is the difference between a person who "walks in the Spirit" and the person that walks according to the "lust of the flesh?" There are six points I would like to emphasize as indicative of the spiritual anointed life.

First, the spiritual anointed life is a life that lives by every word that proceeds from the mouth of God (*Deut. 8:3*). We are not to base our beliefs, purposes, and meaning of life on what others think or believe to be true, but on the Word of God. In order to do this, we must read and study the Word so that we know what it says.

Second, the spiritual anointed life is a life that inclines its ears to hear and obey God's Word (*Isa. 55:3*). The Bible says we must not only be hearers of the Word but doers also (*Jas. 1:23*).

Third, the spiritual anointed life is a life that has the Spirit of God in him or her (*Eze. 37:14*). When we are filled with God's Spirit, we mind the things of God. By that I mean that we are spiritually-minded and are under the influence of the Holy Spirit. Being spiritually-minded is a state of being, not a temporary fix that we encounter during spiritual meetings or services, but a continual abiding of His presence. When our daily lives reflect the fruit of the Spirit, (love, joy, peace, patience, goodness, kindness, meekness, faith and self-control) we can be sure that the Spirit of God is abiding there.

Fourth, the spiritual anointed life is a life that is dead to sin but alive to God (***Rom. 8:10; Gal. 2:20***). How do we know if we are dead to sin? We no longer mind the things of the flesh. We are not absorbed or consumed by the things of this world. If most of our time is spent in making money, shopping, preoccupation with fashion and amusements and find ourselves spending very little or no time with God, then we are probably not dead to sin, but alive to the flesh.

Fifth, the spiritual anointed life is a life lived only to please and glorify the Lord (***Phil. 1:21***). Our thoughts, plans, activities, hopes, and aspirations should be completely wrapped up and centered in Jesus. Our daily existence has its beginning and end around our Savior.

Finally, the spiritual anointed life is a life that exhibits love towards mankind regardless of their education, nationality, rank or position in life (***1 Jn. 3:14***). Love is displayed in acts of kindness, empathy, and genuine concern for one another. Walking in the Spirit is much more than keeping the commandments; it's all about living out the principles in our day to day walk. It actually boils down to how we treat one another. If we are unloving, unkind, unforgiving, and unsympathetic to the needs of others, we are not walking in the Spirit. If we find ourselves tearing down or taking advantage of individuals to get ahead, we are walking in darkness no matter how much time we spend in church, pay tithe or profess that we have faith in Jesus.

The direct opposite of walking in the Spirit is walking according to the "lust of the flesh." The "lust of the flesh" is a carnal life in which evil desires are continuously ready to express themselves in some type of bodily form. It is the natural tendency towards evil (**Ps. 51:5**). In order to walk in accordance with the spiritual anointed life, we must put to death the fleshly lust. The Bible says these "works of the flesh" are adultery, fornication, impurity, public indecency, idolatry, sorcery, hatred, contentions, jealousies, outbursts of anger, selfish ambitions, strife, false doctrines, envy, murder, drunkenness, and revelries (**Gal. 5:19-21**). How is it possible to mortify these fleshly desires and tendencies? I sometimes feel like Paul when he expressed his frustration concerning the vicious war against the carnal and the spiritual life. In the **Message** Bible, Paul's frustration reads like this:

What I don't understand about myself is that I decide one way, but then I act another, doing things I absolutely despise. So if I can't be trusted to figure out what is best for me and then do it, it becomes obvious that God's command is necessary. But I need something more! For if I know the law but still can't keep it, and if the power of sin within me keeps sabotaging my best intentions, I obviously need help! I realize that I don't have what it takes. I can will it, but I can't do it. I decide to do good, but I don't really do it; I decide not to do bad, but then I do it anyway. My decisions, such as they are, don't result in actions. Something has gone wrong deep within me and gets the better of me every time. It happens so regularly that it's predictable. The moment I decide to do good, sin is there to trip me up. I truly delight in God's commands, but it's pretty obvious that not all of me joins in that delight. Parts of me covertly rebel, and just when I least expect it, they take charge. I've tried everything and nothing helps. I'm at the end of my rope. Is there no one who can do anything for me? Isn't that the real question? The answer, thank God, is that Jesus Christ can and does. He acted to set things right in this life of contradictions where I want to serve God with all my heart and mind, but am pulled by the influence of sin to do something totally different (Rom. 7:15-25).

There are also six points I'd like to suggest that will help us in the war against the "works of the flesh:"

1) **Cast it out! Deny yourself!** (*Mt. 5:29; 18:8*) These words of Jesus go far beyond the actual mutation of the eye and the hand. The meaning is much more complex than simply plucking out the eye or cutting off the hand. Christ is suggesting that we look at the motive behind our actions. Our outward acts generally start in the mind, which can be triggered by what we see, hear, taste, smell, and touch. We must cut out those things that prompt us to feed our deadly carnal desires. Perhaps we should

start with an inventory of what we watch on cable TV/DVD, at the cinema and/or on the Internet **(Pause and Reflect.)** Anything that the Bible lists as "works of the flesh," should be cast out.

2) **Crucify the old man (Rom. 6:6).** Make a conscious decision to renounce your evil past—that old man, in its corrupt and sinful condition. You are now a new creature in Christ Jesus and His Spirit dwells in you.

3) **Put to death the deeds of the body through the power of the Holy Spirit (Rom. 8:13).** This is a continuous process of not yielding to bodily impulses, desires, or appetites but rather yielding to the power of the Holy Spirit. Learn to cooperate with the Holy Spirit. We are to live to please and glorify God in every area of our lives.

4) **Make no provisions for the flesh, to fulfill its lusts (Rom. 13:14).** Let us not give any forethought to our depraved appetites, desires or cravings. Overindulgent of physical or emotional wants triggers the unholy passions that we need to put to death. Live simple and balanced lives.

5) **Abstain from fleshy lust (1 Pet. 2:11).** Although we live in a degenerate age, we are to shun the contact of evil influences. It is imperative that we guard the mind from hearing, seeing or watching anything that is against the principles of God.

6) **Walk daily, in the Spirit (Gal. 5:16).** We need to daily surrender ourselves to God and ask daily for willingness to obey through His power. This will enable us to

live the spiritual anointed life that God has ordained for us to live.

It is so wonderful to know that we are not saved by the works (law) that we do, but we are saved through grace. As Christians saved by the blood of the Lamb, we live in and through the righteousness of Christ. This means that we have a close relationship with Him and His works of obedience will be seen through us as proof of a genuine spiritual anointed life. The question we might want to ask ourselves is "have I accepted the saving, anointing grace of Christ in my life?"

In conclusion, a crucial part of the spiritual anointed life is taking the time out to study the Word of God, prayer and sharing God's love with others. I would like to share 4 steps to understanding and rightly dividing the Word of Truth:

1) Open your mind up to receive truth; open mindedness is imperative to understanding truth. We cannot approach the Word of God with our own preconceived ideas and opinions.

2) Pray for understanding, wisdom and guidance through the power of the Holy Spirit.

3) Compare scriptural texts with other scriptural texts on any given topic. "Precept upon precept and line upon line" (***Isa. 28: 9-10***). Go through various texts (from Genesis to Revelation) on a particular subject (i.e. resurrection); look up the text that gives meaning and understanding on the subject of resurrection. This takes time but it very

rewarding and it gives you a better under-standing of the Word of God.

4) Apply the principles of truth that you have gained to your everyday life experiences. Act on the knowledge acquired through your study. Understanding and knowledge without practical application is useless.

Chapter VII

The Emotional Anointed Life

John 8:8-12 — And again He stooped down and wrote on the ground. Then those who heard it, being convicted by their conscience went out one by one, beginning with the oldest even to the last. And Jesus was left alone, and the woman standing in the midst. When Jesus had raised Himself up and saw no one but the woman, He said to her,"Woman, where are those accusers of yours? Has no one condemned you?" She said,"No one, Lord"' and Jesus said to her, "Neither do I condemn you; go and sin no more." Then Jesus spoke to them again, saying, "I am the light of the world. He who follows Me shall not walk in darkness, but have the light of life."

The emotional anointed life can be described as one in which a person displays healthy emotions in that he or she is able to manage stress and convey positive emotions such as joy, love, peace, and affection towards others. Such an individual is also able to appropriately manage negative emotions such as anger and fear, and is also capable of handling the day to day challenges. Emotionally anointed people are secure within themselves and capable of producing and maintaining satisfying relationships.

If the truth were told, many of us lack the emotional stability described above. We all have been abused, misused, or hurt emotionally, at some point in our lives. Some of us feel trapped in our own skin with feelings and emotions that are out of control. Others have tried to form intimate relationships, which have failed miserably. Emotionally, some of us are wound up so tightly that we are about to explode or go into a rage at the tiniest provocation. How can we get our emotions and feelings under control and experience the emotional anointed life that God longs for us to have? Five steps may aide in getting our emotions under control:

Step 1 – Admit that all of us have some type of "emotional baggage." All of us are sinners, saved by grace; therefore we all have experienced struggles, fears, hurt, pain, losses, and disappointments. It doesn't matter who we are; the consequences of sin have taken its toll on us emotionally. We must admit that we all have or had emotional damaged goods. The apostle Paul, counsels us "to put away all bitterness, wrath, anger clamor, evil speaking and spite" (**Eph. 4:31**).

Step 2 – Know that God is willing to take our emotional baggage and give us His unconditional love, peace, and joy (emotional freedom). Jesus came to this world for the purpose of saving sinners (of whom I am chief). He says that nothing or nobody can separate us from His love (**Rom. 8:35-39**). His love is unconditional and everlasting; so "if God is for us who can be against us?" "He who did not spare His own Son, but delivered Him up for us all, how shall He not with Him also freely give us all things?" (**Rom. 8: 31-32**)

Step 3 – Except God's emotional healing by faith not feelings. We are to walk by faith not by feelings. Although we tend to believe only what we see, feel or touch, this world and its surroundings are not what we should be focusing on for they will surely pass away. What we should focus on and claim by faith are the promises in the Word of God. "Do not love the world or the things in the world. If anyone loves the world, the love of the Father is not in him. For all that *is* in the world; the lust of the flesh, the lust of the eyes, and the pride of life; is not of the Father but is of the world. And the world is passing away, and the lust of it; but he who does the will of God abides forever" (**1Jn. 2:15-17**). The lust of the flesh, the lust of the eyes, and the pride of life are directly linked with our feeling and emotions. Unfortunately, these emotions and feelings can be very deceitful especially if we depend on them as a barometer of the realities of life. These feelings and emotions must give way to the realities that are in Jesus

Christ our Savior and Healer. Whatever He says, He is able to bring it to pass.

Step 4 – Walk in your new emotional anointed life!

We need to act as if we are healed because "By His stripes we are healed." Stop speaking doubt or acting out those negatives emotional behaviors. Begin to talk to yourself and say "I am free from the emotional drama in my life." I no longer need to rehearse my negative past or act on feelings of insecurity because of former hurts or disappointments. I choose to walk in the love, joy, and peace that God has promised me, and I no longer react to slights or insults from those that are not free from their issues. I choose to love, respect, and show affection to others even if it is not reciprocated.

Step 5 – Allow the Holy Spirit to teach you how to guard the avenues of your mind and heart. *Proverbs 4:23* states that we should "Keep your (our) heart with all diligence, for out of it spring the issues of life." The fact is that there are unsafe and dangerous people in the world, unhealthy situations and environments, and unwise decisions and courses of action we can pursue; however, we must allow the Holy Spirit to teach us how to become wise and discerning and to make choices that promote rather than demote our emotions. Pray everyday for discernment.

Step 6 – Pray daily for the "fruit of the Spirit" to be manifested in your life. Memorize and claim the spiritual fruit in *Galatians 5: 22, 23* "but the fruit of the Spirit is love, joy, peace, longsuffering, kindness, goodness, faithfulness, gentleness, self-control. Against such there is no

Law." Recite it every day and ask God to help you to possess the fruit of the Spirit in your day to day experiences.

These steps are depicted in the story of the emotionally distraught woman who was caught in the very act of adultery. I don't know how she got to this point in her life, in that she was being used and exploited sexually, but here she was an emotional wreck—literally—looking for love in all the wrong places. When the Scribes and Pharisees brought her to Jesus, to get Him to agree with the stoning process, He acted as if He didn't hear their accusations against the woman. He simply began writing something on the ground. I believe He was writing down their little sinful escapades that they thought were hidden. Then Jesus made a statement, in which the truth was already known. He said, "He who is without sin among you, let him throw a stone at her first" (*Jn. 8:7*). Needless to say, not one stone was thrown because "all have sinned and come short of the glory of God" (*Rom. 3:23*).

What I like most about this story is when Jesus asked the woman caught in adultery, "Where are your accusers and those who would condemn you?" She replied that there was no one to accuse or condemn her. Then the Kings of Kings and the Lord of Lords said to her that He didn't condemn her either but she was to walk in her emotional healing and sin no more. Jesus not only pardoned the sins of this woman, but he also released her from her emotional addictions and baggage.

Although it is my belief that God heals or delivers when we ask by faith, the healing or deliverance may not be manifested instantly or at that moment in time; however, the healing has already been declared through the stripes of our Lord and Savior. Most of the time deliverance is a process. As we begin walking in our healing the desired results will surely come. Nevertheless, I am so glad that Jesus is the same yesterday, today and forever. What he did for this woman such a long time ago, He will do for you and me.

There is a key element of the anointed emotional life that I am compelled to address: sexual immorality. In other words, some of the emotional baggage many carry is the result of participating in various forms of sexual immorality—counterfeit ways of trying to experience the happiness, affection, and love we all want and need. The Bible offers ample counsel regarding sexual immorality. Because of the multitude of individuals, both Christians and non-Christians, who are caught up in all forms of sexual immorality, I want to elaborate on some of that Biblical wisdom because it is key to experiencing an anointed emotional life.

The texts found in *1 Corinthians 6:12-20* emphasizes how we are to glorify God physically, mentally, spiritually and emotionally. The **Amplified** Bible rendition of this text reads like this:

> *12Everything is permissible (allowable and lawful) for me; but not all things are helpful (good for me to do, expedient and profitable when considered with other things).*
> *Everything is lawful for me, but I will not become the slave of anything or be brought under its power. 13Food [is intended] for*

*the stomach and the stomach for food,
but God will finally end [the functions of]
both and bring them to nothing. The body
is not intended for sexual immorality, but
[is intended] for the Lord, and the Lord [is
intended] for the body [to save, sanctify,
and raise it again]. ¹⁴And God both raised
the Lord to life and will also raise us up by
His power. ¹⁵Do you not see and know that
your bodies are members (bodily parts) of
Christ (the Messiah)? Am I therefore to take
the parts of Christ and make [them] parts of
a prostitute? Never! Never! ¹⁶Or do you not
know and realize that when a man joins
himself to a prostitute, he becomes one
body with her? The two, it is written, shall
become one flesh. ¹⁷But the person who is
united to the Lord becomes one spirit with
Him. ¹⁸Shun immorality and all sexual
looseness [flee from impurity in thought,
word, or deed]. Any other sin which a
man commits is one outside the body, but
he who commits sexual immorality sins
against his own body. ¹⁹Do you not know
that your body is the temple (the very
sanctuary) of the Holy Spirit Who lives
within you, Whom you have received [as a
Gift] from God? You are not your own, ²⁰You
were bought with a price [purchased with a
preciousness and paid for, made His own].
So then, honor God and bring glory to Him
in your body.*

Notice how the various dimensions of the
healthy anointed life interact with one another.

Our thoughts turn into actions, and actions result in consequences—both emotional and spiritual. In verse 12, Paul's discussion begins with the limitations of liberality and the need for self-control. In an age where self-control is a byword and in which most of society is out of control, sexually (and in other ways), there is a desperate need to obtain and maintain balance, and in some cases, abstinence in our lives. Verse 13 continues with the logic that foods were made for man to eat and enjoy, and the stomach was made by God to properly digest the food. Even though God supplies the food, we are not at liberty to eat whatever we desire, how much we desire or whenever we desire, to the detriment of our health. We must practice self-control, even with the healthiest foods, in order to experience *"the healthy anointed life."*

In addition, Paul states that the body (physical) was not created for sexual immorality, but is to be devoted for the purpose of glorifying the Lord. He offers arguments against sexual immorality, but before I list these six arguments I'd like to clarify what is considered sexual immoral behavior. The general term used for all forms of illicit sexual behavior is *fornication*. Fornication is derived from the Greek word *"porneia"* which includes premarital sex, adultery, homosexuality, incest, harlotry, and any other type of unlawful sex.[1] What is interesting is that all of these types of sexual immorality begins with the prefix "porn" in the Greek. In today's vernacular, the word "porn" means creative activity (writing, pictures, films, etc.) and the depiction of explicit sexual matter for the purpose of sexual excitement. Notice that the term applies to the depiction of the act rather than the act itself. What is also interesting is that the Greek word for harlotry *"porneuo"* (porn-yoo-o) means "to act the harlot," which literally means to indulge in unlawful lust or practice fornication. So in actuality sexual immorality (fornication) = unlawful lust and/or the act of committing illicit sexual intercourse.[2]

Whether a person watches "porno" pictures, movies, etc. or actually performs the illicit sexual act, he or she is, in fact, committing fornication. This concept may be hard to digest so I would ask you to seriously study and pray for the guidance of the Holy Spirit.

Now back to the six arguments against "porneia" or sexual immorality:

#1 – The body was not made for sexual immorality but for the Lord (*vs. 13*). The Lord created our bodies to glorify Him. We are not to misuse His gift of life by indulging in any forbidden practices that harm the body, mind and spirit. Our passions, emotions, and affections should be under the control of the Holy Spirit, not under the control of our own sinful desires.

#2 – God raised up our Lord Jesus Christ from the dead and will raise us up by His power (*vs. 14*). When God raised Christ from the dead, He raised Him up with a glorified body; a body that was perfectly holy, pure and immortal. Likewise, by faith the believer will also, someday very soon, be resurrected with glorified bodies. As believers in the Most High God, shouldn't we by the power of God keep ourselves from any form of degrading practices since Jesus has raised us up to walk in newness of life *(Rom. 6:4)*? Absolutely!

#3 – We are members of Christ (the Body of Christ).

Believers are united to Christ and it is unimaginable that we would dare to take the Body of Christ and defile it by sexual immorality. The act of fornication joins the body to a whore (male or female) and degrades the mind, body, and soul of the individual(s) involved. As members of Christ we have an obligation to abstain from anything that could sever our union with Christ.

#4 – Fornication is different than other sins because it violates the sacredness of our own bodies *(vs. 18)*. Our bodies are sacred because we have joined them as members of Christ and also the marriage is sacred because it represents the oneness or union between Christ and the Church (members of the Body of Christ). The act of fornication is unique in that it is a sin that destroys the body, because the body is direct agent (or tool) through which the sin is committed. Fornication is especially heinous because the body is not only used as the instrument to commit the sin, but it is also the object against which the sin is committed. Think of it this way; when a man and woman commit to marriage, they become "one flesh" *(Gen 2:24)*—one body, so to speak. If a husband commits adultery, he commits the act against his own body (his wife) because the two are one. Essentially, the body (the husband) is not only the agent of the act, but the body (the union of both man and wife) is also the victim of

the act. The same occurs in the spiritual union with Christ. This is a double crime and will inflict severe damage to the marriage relationship and, more importantly, to our spiritual relationship with Christ.

#5 – Our bodies are the temple of the Holy Spirit *(vs. 19)*.

Since our bodies are consecrated temples of the Holy Spirit, they should be kept clean and undefiled. When we commit physical and spiritual fornication, we are in fact sinning against the Father, the Son and the Holy Spirit.

#6 – We are not our own *(vs. 19, 20)*.

Since God is both our Creator and Redeemer, and we are God's property, we have no right to do as we please. Every area or dimension of our life (physical, spiritual, mental, emotional, social, and occupational) belongs to God, for the expressed purpose of glorifying Him.

Sexual immorality goes against God's clearly expressed will. It damages our relationships with the parties that are involved and, most importantly, with our Maker. Besides being a sinful indulgence, abuse or relationship, its consequences are devastating; in the form of guilt, shame, remorse, and anxiety to physical diagnosis of diseases such as herpes, HIV and AIDS. The best way to protect ourselves from such overwhelming, adverse effects of sexual immorality is to adhere to the Biblical principles such as purity, self-control and sexual abstinence outside of marriage.

Many individuals have become caught up in the world of sexual perversions, addictions, and immorality, but God is able to help break this sexual depravity that is prevalent in our society today. It may also be necessary for an individual to seek help from a competent professional to unpack and experience healing from their "emotional baggage." This is especially so when the baggage was collected from a traumatic event or series of events (i.e. various forms of abuse, including sexual abuse or child maltreatment). It may also be necessary when the factors contributing to the person's emotional baggage has extended over a long period of time (i.e. there may be adults who have yet to experience a safe, nurturing, healthy relationship from their childhood to the present). It is often difficult for such persons to do their own unpacking without the help of a Christian, compassionate, and competent professional. There are many Christian counseling services that are available to help break these emotional issues. One that I highly suggest and recommend is Training for Transformation (www. trainingfortransformationinc.org/home.aspx).

Chapter VIII

The Social Anointed Life

> *Psalm 29:1 (NLT)* — *The earth is the* LORD's, *and everything in it.* *The world and all its people belong to Him.*

The above text summarizes the social anointed life in terms of our relationships, community and environment. It states that God is the Divine Ownership of our world, which includes everything in it and everyone who lives on it.

Relationships

From the beginning of time, God had established "a continuing attachment or association between persons"[1] (relationships). In *Genesis 2:18* the LORD God said, "*It is not good that man should be alone; I will make him a helper comparable to him.*" God intentionally created companionships among the animals so that Adam could realize his need for a suitable companion for himself. The fact is that God created us all as social creatures. This socialization, put in place by God, is key to self-worth and well-being. This Biblical concept is backed by current research which suggests that there is significant health benefits associated with social relationships. By contrast, isolation results in a higher mortality rate.[2]

I believe that people should have at least one close godly relative or friend in their life to whom they are accountable. This is necessary for social and spiritual growth. We don't always see ourselves as others do, and we need at least one person who we give permission to speak the truth, even if what he or she says convicts us of negative behaviors or praises us for what we do well. I am privileged to have such persons in my life. I give them license to get in my business— which means they can critique, praise, pray, pry, and make judgments in my life. I don't always like what they say, but I respect their opinions. Our response should be to listen with an open mind, reflect on what is being communicated, and pray for the guidance of the Holy Spirit. The Bible gives specific instructions regarding godly counsel (***Prov. 11:14; 12:15; 15:22***). It is of no profit if we listen to and hear the godly counsel of a friend or relative and then ignore it or fail to act on it. The wise individual heeds the godly counsel of God and those through whom God speaks.

Having that type of relationship I just described will take you out of your comfort zone and boost your spiritual and social growth like nothing else can. I believe this to be an intricate part of the social anointed life.

An English poet coined a famous but very true line that said "no man is an island." Nothing done under the sun is done singularly (without the aid of someone or something). It takes two people to produce another person. Throughout our lives there is a constant influence that is generated by every individual—be it good or bad. At our death, we are dependent on someone to bury us. This adage holds true in the spiritual realm as well. Consider again, **Genesis 1:26** (1st part). God said "let us make man in our image in our likeness." Notice the plurality of this statement (us, our). God (in the form of the Father, Son and Holy Spirit) was the creative agent in forming humanity. The Biblical record also states that God created them (male and female) in the image of God (Father, Son and Holy Spirit); so from the beginning, God created man (male and female) to interrelate with one another and, most importantly, with their God.

Without question, relationships between male and female, at times, can be very rewarding and satisfying. Unfortunately, these relationships can often be equally discouraging and perplexing— partly because we lack the skill on how we relate to the opposite sex and how to set appropriate boundaries as we interrelate. God created the male female relationship to complement each other and as a way to reflect His image. There are seven basic spiritual and social principles that can aid in relating more effectively in our relationship with members of the opposite sex:[4]

1) Establishing a relationship with God is fundamental in the formation of relationships between male and female. I do not believe anyone is capable of making a wise choice in whom to associate with without having a firm relationship with God and heeding the promptings of the Holy Spirit.

2) Relationships should be based on respect for the other and appreciation of the various differences (*Eph. 4:2, NCV*). Both male and female are made in the image of God and therefore neither is superior or inferior to one another although they may have different roles.

3) Relationships with the opposite sex should be chosen wisely. Christian male/female relationships should not only take on the name of Christian but live out the principles in his/her life.

4) Friendships between the opposite sexes should be clearly defined, to avoid misunderstandings and frustration for either of the parties (i.e. "just friends" can take on different meanings that are based on the individual concept of the term).

5) If one is interested in a special friendship that may possibly evolve into a permanent relationship, the most effective way to pursue this alternative, would be within a context of community. This can best be accomplished by involvement with a community of believers. I personally believe that friendships should grow out from the Body of Christ and not necessarily from a one-on-one interaction. A person is able to

observe a great deal more about another individual in a group setting than hanging out one-on-one.

6) Emotional and physical intimacy without marriage is inadvisable. Keep physical involvement in check and in line with Biblical principles (*1 Thess. 4:1-8*).

7) Never read into what the opposite sex is thinking about you based on a kind gesture, pleasant look or slight attention.

Unfortunately, the current socially acceptable interaction between males and females seems to be one in which there are neither boundaries nor expectations of accountability. No clear lines between the appropriate and the inappropriate are drawn, and the sacredness of the male female relationship has been diluted to make way for the trend of *"friends with benefits (casual sexual relationships without emotional involvement)."* Engaging in such an arrangement is—for lack of a better description—grand theft. Think in terms of a bank account. When you have an account, you deposit and withdraw currency (money) as needed—as appropriate. When your funds are depleted, there is no more currency against which you can do necessary business transactions. In much the same way, when we engage in sacred, appropriate, relationships (male and female), there are emotional and mental currency being invested in the relationship. When both parties are vested in or have a vested interest in the relationship, both will make deposits of currency (emotional, mental, and spiritual) to secure each other's holistic investment. On the other hand, when neither party has a vested interest, or only one party does, odds are that withdrawals will far exceed deposits, and that account will become depleted, perhaps overdrawn, and unbalanced. This is true of the relationships built on the friends-with-benefits model—and the damage done can often be irreparable.

Community

The concept of relationships becomes adamantly clear when we think of community and what that really means. According to Webster (dictionary), community is defined as individuals living together as a smaller unit within a larger unit with like interests, work or traditions for the purpose of fellowship and friendly association. Spiritually speaking, God is the originator of community because God, in essence, is community and we were created in His image to reflect that sphere of community—which is our fundamental purpose. The basic purpose of community can be summarized as the exhibition of love to man and to God. In other words, community, in its simplicity, is to love and to be loved by others. Have you ever wondered why God created man? You guessed it—for COMMUNITY! You see, in order to be community we are dependent upon one another to love and be loved. Most importantly, all are connected by God's all- encompassing love. As Christians, we have been redeemed by the blood of the Lamb! In view of the fact that through the love of God we are all connected, and that by His grace we are redeemed, there are certain responsibilities, duties, and privileges we should have towards one another that come as a result of this knowledge. These expectations for the Christian that embrace the social anointed life is laid out in **Ephesians 4:1-6 (Amplified)**.

¹I THEREFORE, the prisoner for the Lord, appeal to and beg you to walk (lead a life) worthy of the [divine] calling to which you have been called [with behavior that is a credit to the summons to God's service, ²Living as becomes you] with complete lowliness of mind (humility) and meekness (unselfishness, gentleness, mildness), with patience, bearing with one another and making allowances because you love one another. ³Be eager and strive earnestly to guard and keep the harmony and oneness of [and produced by] the Spirit in the binding power of peace. ⁴[There is] one body and one Spirit—just as there is also one hope [that belongs] to the calling you received— ⁵[There is] one Lord, one faith, one baptism, ⁶One God and Father of [us] all, Who is above all [Sovereign over all], pervading all and [living] in [us] all.

1. **We are to walk worthy of our social anointing.** This anointing is exemplified "with lowliness (humility of mind) and gentleness, with longsuffering (patience) bearing with one another in love. I believe that the phrase "bearing with each other" takes on a dual meaning. It refers to one's behavior, standards of conduct or social interactions with one another, and it also refers to a means of support or upholding each other during life's challenges with love and understanding.

2. **We are to keep the unity of the Spirit in the bond of peace.** This oneness is exercised in the body of Christ. There are many members of the body, but there is only one body which further emphasizes the fact that we are not loners but we are connected to the family of God.

Environment

As stated earlier in chapter one, God created a perfect environment for our first parents to live in. God told them to rule over or to "have dominion over the fish of the seas, over the birds of the air and over the cattle, over all the earth and over every creeping thing that creeps on the earth" (*Gen. 1:26, last part*). We see in this text that God gave the responsibility to man to take care of the earth and the things in the earth. Also, in **Genesis 2:15** God put Adam and Eve in the Garden of Eden and told them "to tend and keep it." "To keep," comes from the Hebrew word "shamar" which means to guard, watch, preserve or observe. God was communicating to the Edenic pair that He wanted them to be good stewards of the things that He made and the provisions that He gave them.

Today, our beautiful world has been polluted and seriously marred by the environmental changes of the earth's composition and man's abuse of the planet earth. Change in the ecosystems (lakes, forests, grasslands, etc.) has caused many variations of the earth's environment resulting in extremes in weather patterns such as excessive heat, cold, flooding, and storms, etc.

Our food choices have played a large part in the depletion of the earth's resources such as water, wildlife, soil and trees. In addition, the earth has experienced abuse from pollution created by smoke, hazardous chemicals, and oil spills, just to name a few. These unfortunate issues have caused great damage to our world and things in the world. So as humans we have not done such a good job with taking care of our world which God created. You may ask, "Is it really my responsibility to care for, preserve and watch over the environment in which I live? Absolutely! Why? Because we are recipients of God's creation. God has lovingly provided everything (water, air, sunlight, food, etc.) we need in order for us to live. In response to all that He has given, shouldn't we at least do what we can to be good stewards of the earth? *(Pause and Reflect.)*

Taken from the famous, or not so famous, event called "Earth Day,"[3] I'm suggesting several ways to care for the environment in which we live:

1. Recycle

Recycling is a very simple, yet efficient, means of saving our environment. I must admit that I was not really completely sold on the idea at first. That was until I met my husband of three years, who religiously recycles everything that he is able to recycle. He has a container for plastics, paper and cans. This drove me crazy at first until I realized that this was a way for me to do my part to help save our environment while providing more economical advantages. A single person who recycles can make a big difference on our environment by eliminating waste in landfills and saving natural resources.

2. Reduce

We accumulate a lot of stuff; perhaps we need to take an inventory of the things we have stored away before we go out and buy new stuff. I believe we waste lots of time and money buying things that are not necessary for us to live comfortably. Reducing the amount of waste we throw out is the key to the conservation of our planet earth. Today, we have so much trash that we are running out of places to store it. As good stewards of God's creation, we must be more conscientious about the things we buy. If we buy only the things we need, and not everything we want, we are taking a giant step towards reducing waste.

3. Reuse

There are many things that we throw away that can be reused in another form. You may ask, "Why is this necessary?" The answer is of course that it helps to save money, time, and natural resources. So let's take a look at what you can reuse. You can reuse paper (cut off partially used printed paper for writing notes or telephone info); glass containers (use to store just about anything); and plastic containers (if you have enough freezer space, fill them up with water and freeze. You can use them later in your cooler at a picnic). As Christians, we cannot forget those who are less fortunate then we are. Instead of throwing things away, we can *"clean um," "fix um" or "repair um,"* and give them away to someone who needs them.

In summary, we can be good stewards of our earth by caring for the environment, conserving resources and contributing natural resources to those that are in need.

Chapter IX

The Occupational Anointed Life

Deuteronomy 28:1-6 — Now it shall come to pass, if you diligently obey the voice of the LORD your God, to observe carefully all His commandments which I command you today, that the LORD your God will set you high above all nations of the earth. And all these blessings shall come upon you and overtake you, because you obey the voice of the LORD your God: Blessed shall you be in the city, and blessed shall you be in the country. Blessed shall be the fruit of your body, the produce of your ground and the increase of your herds, the increase of your cattle and the offspring of your flocks.

> *Blessed shall be your basket and your kneading bowl.*
> *Blessed shall you be when you come in, and blessed shall you be when you go out.*

I am truly convinced that the occupational anointed life is based primarily on the other aspects of the healthy anointed life. For example, if the spiritual part of us is unhealthy then the occupational part of us will most likely mirror the unconsecrated inner self. God is always in the blessing business but a major part of receiving His blessings are based on our obedience to Him spiritually, physically, emotionally, socially and intellectually. When these areas are fully committed to Him, the results can be described as "blessings coming in and blessings going out." We are blessed and highly favored; in return, we are able to bless others with the resources we have been blessed with.

Occupational health emphasizes our choice of work, job satisfaction, career endeavors and personal performance. More importantly, the occupational anointed life considers God's economy system. This system is based on spiritual principles such as obedience, stewardship, and benevolence. It is God who gives us the ability to gain wealth whether through our work choices or investment resources. It is God who gives talents and gifts to be used for His glory, and it is God who gives us health and strength everyday to perform the various tasks at our place of employment. The Bible says that all the silver and gold belongs to God and the cattle on a thousand hills are His. In fact, everything belongs to God. Even our money that we acquire from being gainfully employed doesn't belong to us. Since God is the ownership of everything including our finances, we should let Him handle all of the resources He has given us. We are just the stewards (managers) of God's resources.

If we want to be directed to the appropriate job choice or career, experience job satisfaction and favor, and be blessed financially; God's economy system can help us encounter the occupational anointed life.

Obedience

The first step to obedience is to surrender everything that we think we own to God. Larry Burkett refers to this as transference of ownership.[1] I expressed this same concept in chapter 8, in which the key text (**Ps. 24:1**) reminds us that *"the earth is the LORD's, and everything in it."* This step takes a lot of prayer because we really believe that all the stuff that we have belongs to us. It doesn't! Once we have made the transfer, then we should ask God for His guidance as to what we should do with the resources He has provided.

One of the principles to being a good steward is tithing. God is so generous that all He asks of us is to give Him a tenth of everything we earn. Although He gives us the other nine-tenths, we must remember that we are only managing what God has given us. Some of us have a real problem with tithing. Somehow, we think that we are losing out when we give God His due. In reality, we are really gaining. In God's infinite economy plan, we give Him the first portion of our increase (the tithe) and He in turn showers us with blessings—not just financial blessings but also spiritual, physical, emotional, social and mental blessings. In fact, He promises us that if we give Him the tithes and offerings, He will bless us so much that we will not have enough room to receive them (**Mal. 3:10**). I say that's a great investment plan!

Stewardship

What is involved in being a good manager? We already emphasized the transference of ownership and the paying of tithes and offerings but I submit to you that being a good steward requires a lot more. You must be a good manager of your time, temple, talents, and testimony as well as you treasures. How we manage our time directly relates to how well we develop our talents, take care of our temple, and initiate our testimony; how we manage our time also directly relates to how successful we are on our jobs or in our careers. Prioritizing our time is the greatest challenge for most of us and, from my point of view, the most important factor in the implementation of the occupational anointed life. As a matter of fact, the management of time has a domino effect on all the other dimensions of the healthy anointed life.

You would think that, as Christians, the amount of time that we give to God through study, meditation, prayer, and witnessing would reflect the commitment that we made to God when we gave our lives to Him. However, current surveys indicate that the average Christian spends less than 10 minutes a day in devotion to God. So that you can really put this in perspective, I'd like to share, in a little more detail, the findings from several surveys on how we spend our time:[2,3,4]

Individual Time Usage Chart

The average lifespan in the US is approximately 77 years, which goes along with the text found in Psalm 90:10 (70-80 yrs.) This is equivalent to:
➢ 28, 000 days ➢ 670, 000 hours ➢ 40, 000, 000 minutes
The average person spends 26 minutes per day getting dressed:
➢ 13 hours per month ➢ 7 days per year ➢ 1 year in a lifetime
The average person works (40) and sleeps (56) 96 hours per week:
➢ 16 days per month ➢ 192 days per year ➢ 40 years in a lifetime
The average person watches 5 hours of TV per day (including weekends):
➢ 150 hours per month ➢ 75 days per year ➢ 15-16 years in a lifetime
The average person spends anywhere between 2-4 hours per day surfing the internet:
➢ 56-120 hours per month ➢ 31-65 days per year ➢ 7-14 years in a lifetime
The average parent interacts in meaningful conversation with their children:
➢ 3-4 minutes per week (does not include conversation such as: clean your room, brush your teeth, go to bed, etc.) ➢ 16 minutes per month ➢ 3 hours and 12 minutes per year
The average "Christian" spends:
➢ Less than 10 minutes each day in devotion to God (including study, prayer, meditation and worship service) ➢ Less than 6 hours per month in devotion to God ➢ Less than 7 months in a lifetime in devotion to God

The results of these surveys, revealed on the above chart, should raise a red flag in the heart of every professed Christian in regard to where our loyalty really lies. This survey indicates that we spend only 7 months in a lifetime in devotion to God, versus 22-30 years in a lifetime watching TV and surfing the Internet. Something is very wrong with this picture. It is obvious that we are spending and investing a lot of time with something, but it isn't God. (*Pause and Reflect.*) All of us need to make a self-assessment to see how we are spending our time than make the necessary adjustments. If your job is such that you are so busy working and making a living and you have little or no time for God, then it is quite probable that you need to change jobs. I personally do not believe that every job that is offered to us is from God and I also don't think that God would give us a job that would make it impossible to devote quality time to Him.

If we were to be honest, we all struggle with the management of time but God has promised that if we put Him first that everything we need will be added to us (*Matt. 6:33*). This includes your finances as well as your talents, temple, and testimony. We must give everything, with time being the currency of life, over to the Lordship of our Savior Jesus Christ.

The **Message** Bible summarizes it this way, "*Don't waste your time on useless work, mere busywork, the barren pursuits of darkness. Expose these things for the sham they are. It's a scandal when people waste their lives on things they must do in the darkness where no one will see. Rip the cover off those frauds and see how attractive they* *look in the light of Christ. Wake up from your sleep, Climb out of your coffins; Christ will show you the light! So watch your step. Use your head. Make the most of every chance you get. These are desperate times (**Eph. 5:11-16**)!"*

Benevolence

There is a direct connection between benevolence and prosperity. The main reasons why God blesses us with employment or a lucrative career, is to supply our needs and the needs of others. God has a work for everyone to do, but we must know that His purpose is not only to bless us but, to bless others also. If we don't bless others, we become selfish and invest our money and resources for that which only benefits ourselves. The Bible makes it clear that we are to lay up treasures for spiritual purposes:

> *"Do not gather and heap up and store up for yourselves treasures on earth, where moth and rust and worm consume and destroy, and where thieves break through and steal. But gather and heap up and store for yourselves treasures in heaven, where neither moth nor rust nor worm consume and destroy, and where thieves do not break through and steal; For where your treasure is, there will your heart be also (**Matt. 6:19-21, Amplified**)."*

Do you want to know where your heart is? Look at your checkbook and where your time is spent. They will tell you exactly what is important and what is not in your life. Take a look right now and see how much you have spent for material blessings versus spiritual blessings. It is important that we take care of our needs and not be a burden on others; however, the principle of giving and receiving is paramount in practicing the occupational anointed life. Should we give only to receive? No! We should give because of a deep spiritual sense of obedience and genuine concern for the welfare of others. But the promises are nevertheless true that if you *"give, you will receive. Your gift will return to you in full—pressed down, shaken together to make room for more, running over, and poured into your lap. The amount you give will determine the amount you get back (**Lk. 6:38, NLT**)."*

You may be saying; "I give a tenth or more of my increase but I am still not experiencing the abundant returns depicted in this verse." Well, perhaps you should look at your motives, attitudes, and expectations. Why would God shower us with blessings if we only use them for material things—a larger house, a big plasma TV, a sports car? Let me ask you a question; does health, strength, having a stable job, children cared for, etc. count as abundant blessings? Or are your expectations summarized in one word "money?' Generally, those who are receiving the bountiful blessings of **Luke 6:38** are individuals who are giving from the heart. They don't demand a blessing or try to bribe God. They give out of the desire to please God, trusting that God is true, faithful, and just and is more than able to supply their every need and even most of their wants. If God doesn't give back according to your expectations, it is not the time to decrease your giving but rather to increase your giving because we know that God is true to His promise and there are some lessons God is trying to teach us on how to be good stewards.

I would like to end this chapter with a few more Biblical guidelines on the occupational anointed life in relationship to God's economy system. These concepts are summarized in **Matthew 25:34-40**:

> *Then the King will say to those on his right, 'Come, you who are blessed by my Father, inherit the Kingdom prepared for you from the creation of the world. For I was hungry, and you fed me. I was thirsty, and you gave me a drink. I was a stranger, and you invited me into your home. I was naked, and you gave me clothing. I was sick, and you cared for me. I was in prison, and you visited me. Then these righteous ones will reply, Lord, when did we ever see you hungry and feed you? Or thirsty and give you something to drink? Or a stranger and show you hospitality? Or naked and give you clothing? When did we ever see you sick or in prison and visit you? And the King will say, I tell you the truth, when you did it to one of the least of these my brothers and sisters, you were doing it to me (**NLT**)!*

Chapter X

Heaven's Wellness System

> *Job 42:10 — And the LORD restored Job's losses when he prayed for his friends. Indeed the LORD gave Job twice as much as he had before.*

After the devil robbed Job of his (physical, mental, spiritual, social, emotional, and occupational) possessions, the Lord restored double-fold everything he lost. What a mighty God we serve! As God restored Job, He has a plan to restore us also. God has provided a heavenly wellness system that will help us reach "the healthy anointed life" that He ordained from the beginning of time. I refer to Heaven's Wellness System as RESTORATION. Each letter stands for health principles that renew and restore vitality and health to the body, mind, and spirit:

Replenish fluids
Exercise
Sunshine
Time (management and balance)
Obedience
Rest (physical and spiritual)
Air (fresh)
Trust in the Lord (with all your heart)
Interest in the general welfare of others
Optimism and Hope
Nutrition

Replenish Fluids

The water that quenched the thirst of our first parents is the same water that is essential for cleansing and detoxing our bodies. Since the body is 65-70% water, it is necessary to drink plenty of water (distilled or purified) for proper body function and to flush out waste. Water is especially important for those individuals who desire to lose weight. During weight loss, the body produces more waste and if the waste or fat is not metabolized, than fat is stored. The following schedule may help you to utilize water more efficiently:

➢ Morning: Upon rising, drink 2-3 glasses of water over a 30-minute period
➢ Noon: Drink 2-3 glasses of water over a 30-minute period
➢ Evening: Drink 2-3 glasses of water, 1 hour before or 1 hour after eating (preferably 3 hours before bedtime)

Water used externally is very beneficial in the prevention of colds and other illnesses, and is also helpful to boost the immune system. One of the easiest ways to do this, is to take a daily hot and cold shower:

1. Start off with warm water than increase temperature gradually until it is hot.
2. Keep the water hot for 2-3 minutes than turn water quickly to cold
3. Keep the water cold for 1 minute.
4. Turn off the water and dry off. For a serious immune boost, repeat steps 2 and 3 three times.

Try the hot/cold shower first thing in the morning. Believe me you won't need that cup of coffee. You will be refreshed and wide awake!

We must also drink freely of the spiritual water (Water of Life) that only Jesus can give. This water is able to quench your thirst to the point where you will never thirst again. Not only that, but this Water of Life becomes a fountain of water that springs up into everlasting life (*Jn. 4:13, 14*). Whatever you are thirsty for, Jesus the Living Water can cleanse, heal, and satisfy your every longing.

Exercise

There are so many reasons why we should exercise that it would take an entire book to fully cover its benefits and positive responses to the body. Exercise is vital essentially because it keeps the temple (our body) fit and suitable for the indwelling of the Holy Spirit. Exercise produces endorphins (hormones) that lifts our spirits and brightens our disposition, giving us a positive outlook on life.[1] Exercise also increases our self-esteem because it enhances our looks (muscle tone, weight management and vitality).

Exercise burns fat and strengthens the heart while increasing the efficiency of the lungs. It saturates the whole body with energy-producing oxygen that protects the body from sickness and disease. If you are struggling with regularity, repetitive exercise stimulates the digestion processes by normalizing the bowels. This is extremely important in terms of how long the food sits in the digestive tract. The longer it takes to digest the food, the greater the risk of disease, especially certain types of cancer. Water, exercise, and a diet high in fiber assist the body in moving the digested foods out of the system quickly and efficiently.

Do you want to look younger and slow down the aging process? Regular exercise is the key to reducing the deterioration of the physical body while restoring your youthful look.[2] It helps to get your spunk back! Overall, exercise benefits your musculoskeletal system (muscles and bones), heart, blood vessels, metabolism, mental process, and stress level. Are you sold on exercise yet? I certainly hope so. Go ahead and get started, especially those of you who have not put exercise in your daily routine. Start out walking ONLY, until your endurance and strength reach a comfortable level. Remember to work into exercise slowly.

I recall what the Apostle Paul says in *1 Corinthians 9:25-27 (Message)*; *"You've all been to the stadium and seen the athletes race. Everyone runs; one wins. Run to win. All good athletes train hard. They do it for a gold medal that tarnishes and fades. You're after one that's gold eternally. I don't know about you, but I'm running hard for the finish line. I'm giving it everything I've got. No sloppy living for me! I'm staying alert and in top condition. I'm not going to get caught napping, telling everyone else all about it and then missing out myself."*

The Apostle Paul elaborates on the spiritual athlete, running to obtain a spiritual crown of eternal life. In order to receive this incorruptible prize we must exercise faith, endurance and self-discipline. What spiritual exercises do you incorporate into your daily regimen in order to become spiritually fit? Why not build spiritual stamina and spiritual muscles by studying God's Word, as well as through prayer, meditation, and witnessing of His goodness.

Sunshine

The benefits from the sun are numerous; however, most are afraid to go out in the sun without some type of sun block, sunglasses, or head covering in order to avoid the harmful rays of the sun. It is true that too much exposure can cause a higher risk of skin cancers, but with a few guidelines we should be able to work our way around the deleterious effects.

Because going out in the sun poses a threat for some, a deficiency of vitamin D is prevalent today, especially for 75% of teens and adults in the U.S.[2] This significant increase is particularly evident among African Americans partly because of the darker complexion which produces more melanin and color pigment in the skin, making it hard to absorb the sunshine in order to manufacture vitamin D. Deficiencies of Vitamin D can lead to health effects such as diabetes, bone disorders, changes in body metabolism and depression.

The benefits of sunshine far outweigh the apparent risk factors. Sunlight creates vitamin D in your skin, enabling you to appropriately utilize calcium which is so crucial for strengthening your bones and teeth. It increases circulation, muscle tone, endurance, and your metabolism. For those who primarily exercise outdoors, sunshine has been shown to build muscles faster than in persons who exercise indoors.[3] Absorbing sunlight boosts the immune system and balances your blood sugar level. For those who struggle with symptoms of PMS, sunlight can add some relief. It also increases the function of the liver and white blood cells to aid in fighting infection. Sunshine promotes healing, a positive outlook, and a sense of well-being.

The following guidelines can help you experience these benefits as well as others of the Creator's wonderful gift of the sun:

1. Avoid putting on creams or oils on the skin, when out in the sun, because they may be converted into harmful substances.
2. Wearing sunglasses or a hat is helpful in shielding the UV rays from your eyes.
3. Keep your exposure to short intervals instead of one long exposure.

4. Begin with 10-15 minutes per day than gradually increase to 30 minutes of sunshine a day.
5. Expose yourself in the sun during times when the UV rays are low; generally, before 10 a.m. and after 5 p.m., especially during the summer months when the days are longer.
6. Never stay in the sun to the point of sunburn.
7. If you exercise outdoors, there is usually no need to bathe in the sun because you are probably getting enough sun.
8. Unless you are in a high-risk category for skin cancer, 10-30 minutes in the sunlight without sunblock is adequate in producing the proper amount of vitamin D in the body.
9. For longer times of sun exposure, choose a natural type of sunblock that does not have the harmful chemicals such as benzophenone, PABA, and triethonoamine in them.[4]
10. Monitor you diet so that you are eating foods that are low in fat.

One of my favorite promises that I claim often, is found in **Malachi 4:2** of the Bible, *"But to you who fear My name The Sun of Righteousness shall arise with healing in His wings; and you shall go out and grow fat like stall-fed calves."* There are many healing properties of the physical sun which God created for His children, but the Sun of Righteousness is none other than Jesus Christ and He alone can bring complete restoration and healing to our sin-sick lives. Thank God for the Son of Righteousness!

Time (Management and Balance)

When I think of time, I immediately wish I had more—more time to do the things I need to do. Do you feel that you have enough time to get things done on a day-to-day basis? What are some of the things that we need more time to accomplish? More hours in the day to work, sleep, develop meaningful relationships, study, prepare healthy meals, worship God, exercise or serve others? Where does all of our time go and why don't we have enough time? Perhaps we all need to take a good look at how we manage our time and whether we have balance in our lives.

Contrary to our dilemma, God says that there is time for everything that we need to experience in this life (**Eccl. 3:1**) and that we must give an account for not using it wisely (**Eccl. 3:17**). The problem, as I see it, is not that we don't have enough time but that we don't make the best use of our time. Look again at the individual time usage chart in Chapter 9. Besides working and sleeping, how is most of our time spent; are we watching TV and spending time on the computer or listening to our favorite CDs? Now we only have 24 hours in a day, so it is very important that we use our time wisely. Some of us work too much, sleep to little, "chill" too much, plan to little, and eat too much, and drink (water) too little. We need balance in our lives.

Biblical Principles on the Use of Time

1. Determine the use of time based on the brevity of life (**Ps. 90:9, 10, 12; Job 8:9; Jas. 4:14**). Life is short and we only have a little while on this earth. Although life is short, time cannot be stopped, stored, or stretched,[5] so we need to make the best of the time on earth so that we can have life eternally.

2. Ask God to give you wisdom in managing your time (**Jas. 1:5; Deut. 32:29; 1 Jn. 2:20**). God is more than willing to give us wisdom to efficiently manage our time, but we must take the time to ask.

3. Knowing God leads to appropriate time management and balance (**2 Pet. 1:5-8; Jn. 4:34; 17:4**). Having a balance is important because being unbalanced in one area can spill over into creating more unbalanced areas in our lives. For example, the tendency to overwork results in imbalances in personal devotion to God, lack of meaningful family time, unwise food choices, lack of sleep, and lack of physical exercise.

4. We must put heavenly responsibilities above earthly duties (**Matt. 6:33; Acts 20:24; Phil. 3:7, 8**). God must take first place in our lives in order for us to have proper balance in our lives. Things that are lasting (meaningful relationships with God, ministry, family, friends) should take priority in our lives. Self-development in terms of excellence in job skills, academic education, personal interests and household

management are important but should not be at the top of your list of priorities.

5. Since time refers to the manner in which we live our lives, we must *"behave ourselves wisely (living prudently and with discretion)"* and walk worthy of God's anointing in and through our lives (**Col. 4:5, Amplified; Eph. 5:15, 16**). A basic principle in conducting ourselves as Kingdom people and exhibiting balance is to abstain from harmful things and to be moderate in healthy things. Some harmful things we must abstain from are intoxicating drugs (mind-altering, inhibition-lowering substances), tobacco (in all it forms), illicit sex, harmful foods, unholy visual images, etc. Some healthy things that we are to be moderate in are: exercise, healthy foods, sexuality with life-partner, acceptable recreation and entertainment.

6. Use our time in being a positive example before the world (**1 Cor.4:1; 9:17-19**). The apostle Paul sums it up this way, *"behave yourselves wisely [living prudently and with discretion] in your relations with those of the outside world (the non-Christians), making the very most of the time and seizing (buying up) the opportunity"* (**Col. 4:5, Amplified**).

It takes time to practice healing sustaining principles and to heal physically, spiritually, intellectually, emotionally, socially, and occupationally, but those who wait (trust, hope, expect) on the Lord shall have renewed (restored) strength. They shall mount up with wings like eagles, run and not be weary and walk and not faint (**Isa. 40:31**).

Time is too short to be squandered in meaningless pursuits and unproductive activities.

Obedience

Restoration does not come about just for the asking or even by just believing. Restoration comes about by asking, believing, and doing those things that God has asked us to do. Vibrant health and wellness of the body, mind, and spirit does not come as a result of chance but by obedience to the laws of health. It is true that we are saved by faith in God and belief that He can do all things, but the fact that we are saved should lead to fruits of obedience (*Jn. 5:14*). When God heals us we have an obligation to be obedient and to walk in that healing by doing those things that preserve health, unless *"a worse thing come upon you."* I believe that God is desirous to heal (*3 Jn. 2*) all who put their faith and trust in Him; however, we must be willing to be healed in the way that God determines and not our perception of how we want to be healed. For example, if God's healing method includes the changing of our lifestyle of unhealthy eating habits, drug addictions, limited sleep habits, or lack of exercise, and our response is that we don't have the time nor the desire to incorporate these changes, how do we expect to be healed?

God does not always heal instantly or miraculously because, most of the time, it is in the waiting that we experience growth and understanding of why we are in need of the healing in the first place. There is a balancing act with these conceptions of faith and obedience. An unknown author stated that the laws of health can no more save us than the symptoms of a disease can cure us. The symptoms don't cure, but they point out our need for the cure. It is God who heals (***Ex. 15:26***) in every dimension of our life, but we must be willing to be healed in obedience to the methods He has designed for our restoration.

Obedience requires that our actions reflect our beliefs. If we know that water, rest, good nutrition, and exercise are good for the body but don't act upon these healthy principles then we are in disobedience to the laws of health. If we know that spiritual devotion to God is needed for spiritual growth but if we don't take the time out to study God's Word, pray, or witness, then we are walking in disobedience. If we know that our minds are to dwell on things that are pure, holy, true, right, etc., but we inundate our minds with movies, videos, and DVDs that break most of laws of God, we are living in disobedience.

The Bible says in ***James 1:25 (Amplified)*** that *"He who looks carefully into the faultless law, the [law] of liberty, and is faithful to it and perseveres in looking into it, being not a heedless listener who forgets but an active doer [who obeys], he shall be blessed in his doing (his life of obedience)."*

Rest (physical and spiritual)

Rest has different connotations, from physical rest to spiritual rest; yet, the physical and spiritual rest are intimately connected.

As we look back, from the beginning, this concept is made apparently clear. In ***Genesis 2:1-3*** we see that after God completed His work of creation, He rested on the seventh day. Did God rest because He was tired? Absolutely not! I believe He rested in contemplation of His completed works. This connotation of *rest* is seen in terms of completeness. The Hebrew word for rest is *shalom*, which as a noun means completeness, peace, health, and prosperity (Strong's Expanded Dictionary). In reflecting again on **Genesis 2:1-3**, we could also conclude that rest refers to the cessation of physical activity; God stopped His physical manifestation of creating the world. Rest is depicted in this sense as being complementary to work. In other words, there is a need to work but there is also a necessity to cease from working. We are able to witness this phenomenon in every living creature including man (generically speaking). As previously emphasized, the word *restoration* means "the act of returning to an original state or condition." Physical and spiritual rest, are primary restorers or components of *"the healthy anointed life."*

Physical rest is probably the most neglected requirement for the restoration of the human body. Although we know that there are numerous benefits and even the fact that God ordained rest for his purposes, most of us seldom get the amount of rest necessary to restore our bodies. What is keeping us from getting the proper amount of rest every night? **(*Pause and Reflect.*)** Is it our jobs, various activities, relationships, ambitions to get ahead and stay ahead, etc.? Whatever it is, we must ask ourselves if it is worth the host of negative effects or problems we encounter or will eventually experience? These negative repercussions may include fatigue, stress, inefficiency, burnout, negative behaviors that can lead to sickness, disease, physical and emotional losses, and premature death—not to mention the fact that we become defective vessels in which God is unable to use to the fullest. Try to get at least 7-8 hours of sleep per night, preferably before 10:00 p.m. People who are tired and sleepy are not at their best and the sleepier they are, the less effective will be their relationships and productivity.

Hebrews 4:9-10 states that just as God rested (in the beginning) from His activity of creating the heavens and the earth to reflect on His works, so we are to cease from our weekly labors and stresses and rest and reflect on the goodness and mercy of the living and powerful God who created us and gives us "every good and perfect gift." Jesus offers us complete rest when He says "come to Me, all you who labor and are heavy laden, and I will give rest." Proper rest every day is beneficial for the physical rest, but God offers us much more; He offers rest for the soul. By faith, through the anointing and restorative power of the Holy Spirit, the promise is given, *"He will give you rest."*

Air (fresh)

Air (fresh and pure) is loaded with many benefits that restore the body, mind, and soul. First of all, it is necessary for us to live; without air we would be dead in about 2-3 minutes. There are however, two types of air: fresh air and stale air. Both will keep you alive, but fresh air will reward you many more health benefits. Pure air enters the cells and carries the oxygen to the rest of the body which aids in healthy cell production and brain function. Clean, fresh air (primarily in natural areas where there are lots of trees, mountains and lakes) is loaded with negative ions. Negative ions are pure oxygen that is free of pollutants and have a high negative charge. Negative ions are abundantly present after a good rain shower or thunderstorm. They produce chemicals in the body that increases your mood and your metabolism which produce more energy. They also decrease stress and help to alleviate depression.

Deep breaths of fresh air help to protect you against germs that may accumulate down in your lungs. If not dispelled, these contaminants can lead to certain types of disease. Deep breathing helps to calm your nerves and aids in sound, restful sleep. In addition, it improves you blood circulation, heart rate, and blood pressure. Finally, breathing in fresh air boosts your immune system and gives you a sense of well-being.[5]

Simple Breathing Techniques to Aid in the Proper Inhalation of Fresh Air

1. Breathe deeply through both your nose and mouth.
2. Breathe in as much air as possible through the motion of protruding your abdomen forward. Do not lift your shoulders up.
3. Hold the air in for approximately 4 seconds.
4. Release the air gradually but thoroughly (approximately 10-15 seconds).
5. Repeat 7-9 times.

In *Job 33:4* (*Amplified*) it states that "[it is] the Spirit of God that made me [which has stirred me up], and the breath of the Almighty that gives me life [which inspires me]."The Lord is the giver of the gift of air and it is up to us to appropriate these benefits to heal, refresh and restore our body, mind, and spirit.

Trust in the Lord

Out of all the components of *heaven's well-ness system*, trusting in God is by far the most important. It is the fundamental construct that holds all the other principles of *"the healthy anointed life"* in place. Basically, if we don't trust God it is impossible for us to apply the ideals of RESTORATION because true restoration begins and ends in faith in a living and trustworthy God. Trusting God is greater than the healthy foods we eat, proper rest, exercise or any potent medicine. It is based on the belief that God has a plan for my life and that He desires only the good for me and He can be trusted to guide and direct every aspect of my life. The Bible says that those who put their trust in God (not man), are blessed (*Jer. 17:7*). We must "trust the Lord with all our heart and lean not on your own understanding; in all your ways acknowledge Him, and He shall direct your paths" (*Prov. 3:5-6*). This point is made painfully clear in *2 Chronicles 16:12-13*; "*In the thirty-ninth year of his reign Asa came down with a severe case of foot infection. He didn't ask God for help, but went instead to the doctors. Then Asa died; he died in the forty-first year of his reign.*" We must not put our trust in the remedy whether a branch of medicine or a branch of a live oak tree,[6] but we must put our trust in God to restore us. We must believe with everything that is within us that God heals.

You might be wondering what it means "to trust" and how you can develop this trust that is so crucial to restoration. First of all, I believe that trust is a fundamental belief or faith in something and someone. But there is more to this. Trust is actually an action word that is based on believing in someone or something that you deem trustworthy. The Free Online Dictionary states that trust is "a firm reliance on the integrity, ability or character of a person or thing" and is related to placing your dependence on that person or thing. Now, when we put our trust in a God who is omniscient, omnipresent, and omnipotent, there should be no doubt that He is capable of handling all of our circumstances and problems. We can run to Him and know that He is our refuge in times of trouble.

Trust should never be based on our feeling and emotions, or even what we see or touch, but in the recognition that God loves us, died for us, and will do anything to save us. We must trust God in the good times and as well as the bad times (in sickness and in health). Yes, as a Christian, you will have trials, tests, and tribulations, but God has promised to see you through each and every one of them. Do you believe that? (**Pause and Reflect.**)

The best way to develop trust in God is to:

❖ Ask God to help you trust Him and give you evidence of that trust;

❖ Spend some quality time everyday in one-on-one devotion with God;

❖ Ask God to reveal Himself to you through the study of His Word;

❖ Make a prayer list of all your concerns and go over them everyday;

❖ Wait on God with expectancy;

❖ Record time and dates of your answered prayers;

❖ Fellowship with other believers for encouragement and affirmation; and

❖ Testify to others about your faith.

A formula for trusting in God may look something like this:

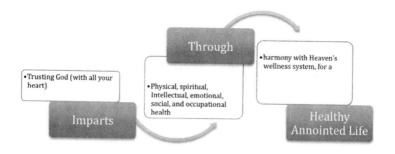

Interest in the Welfare of Others

One of the most powerful words in the world today is "give." Yet, for some of us, it often is one of the hardest things for us to do. Why? Because we are self-focused—a condition that has plagued the human race since sin entered the world. Do you want to be blessed and healed of your issues and circumstances? Then give. Give your life fully to God. Give to those who are less fortunate than you. Give your time, talents, treasures, temple, and testimony to the service of God and man. Not only does giving benefit the recipient, but several scientific studies suggests that giving reduces mortality, adolescent depression and suicide risk, stress, and anxiety.[7]

A word that describes *interest in the welfare of others* is altruism. According to the Merriam Webster dictionary, "altruism is an unselfish regard for or devotion to the welfare of others." Interest in the welfare of others is synonymous with being a Christian. You cannot have one without the other. Biblically, there is an intimate connection between concern for others and health and healing (**Isa. 58:6-8**). True religion is this, "*to loose the bonds of wickedness, to undo the bands of the yoke, to let the oppressed go free, and that you break every [enslaving] yoke? Is it not to divide your bread with the hungry and bring the homeless poor into your house—when you see the naked, that you cover him, and that you hide not yourself from [the needs of] your own flesh and blood? Then shall your light break forth like the morning, and your healing (your restoration and the power of a new life) shall spring forth speedily; your righteousness (your rightness, your justice, and your right relationship with God) shall go before you [conducting you to peace and prosperity], and the glory of the Lord shall be your rear guard.*"(**Amplified**)

In addition to being a Christian characteristic (**Rom. 12:13**), altruism is beneficial to one's personal health. There is actually a "healing power in doing good"[8] for the benefit of others. Giving to others is said to be the best medicine because it helps the ills of this life. Results of significant research flaunted in Allen Luks' studies, on the health benefits of helping others, includes:

> ➤ Decrease in the effects of mental and physical diseases or disorders
> ➤ Reduced mortality rate (*According to Post & Neimark, "Helping friends, relatives and neighbors, along with providing emotional support to a spouse, reduces mortality although receiving the same kind of help does not."*)
> ➤ Release of endorphins (hormones that produce exhilaration or a sense of liveliness) thereby reducing stress and anxiety
> ➤ Decrease in feelings of depression, isolation, hopelessness and worthlessness
> ➤ Greater optimism and a more positive outlook on life
> ➤ Diminished negative behaviors such as anger and hostility
> ➤ Strengthening of the immune system
> ➤ Lowered risk of heart disease and helps to combat cancer

There is a song that conveys the message presented in this section; it goes something like this, "we will know that they are Christians by their love." Love to whom?—God and our fellow man.

Optimism

Dietrich Bonhoeffer, a former German Lutheran Pastor, once wrote that "the essence of optimism is that it takes no account of the present, but it is a source of inspiration, of vitality and hope where others have resigned; it enables a man to hold his head high, to claim the future for himself and not to abandon it to his enemy." Regardless of obstacles that you presently face, keep looking up with faith and hope that everything will work out if you don't give in or give up. We must not buy into the enemy's lies that "its over, you are a failure, or you can't be healed." Stop speaking defeat! Speak victory! Speak healing! Speak prosperity over your mind, body and spirit (**3 Jn. 2**)! Focus on the God who heals and restores! Focus on the Cross (by His stripes we are healed)! Focus on God's everlasting love! Focus on and rejoice in every promise that proceeds from the mouth of God (His Word)! The Bible makes a declaration to "rejoice in the Lord always. Again I will say, rejoice (**Phil. 4:6**)."

You may be asking yourself, "How can I be positive or an optimist when everything is going wrong?—There are money challenges, health problems, relationship issues, sin addictions and unfavorable circumstances in my life. Am I, supposed to rejoice, when all of this is going on?" Yes, because we know that God has promised to get us through each and every circumstance and that these situations are only temporary for the one who puts his faith and trust in God. We must believe that **all** things work together for good to them that love the Lord.

One of the reasons why we are not as optimistic as we should be is because we too often dwell on the negative. We keep ourselves so busy with the mundane things of this world that we are unable to focus on spirituals things which brings about hope. Our relationship with God helps us to be positive and to experience hope even during stressful times and circumstances. We are also admonished in **Philippians 4:8**, to think on things that are true, noble, just, pure, lovely, of a good report and that are virtuous and praise-worthy. If we think on these spiritual themes, I believe we would have a more positive outlook on life.

Nutrition

What we eat today—walks and talks with us tomorrow. The food that we eat directly affects our physical, spiritual, and mental makeup. Food brings nourishment to our bodies via the blood, tissues, and bones in order to keep us strong and healthy. If we eat the wrong kinds of food our bodies react by becoming sick (acutely) or diseased (chronically). I hope that you will agree with me that there are indeed some types of foods that are just not good for us. In fact, there are some foods that can clog our system, over time, causing untimely deaths to millions. The food we eat can also affect our brains thereby influencing our mental processes. Let's look at what a healthy diet should look like. Perhaps we should go back to the beginning (a very good place to start).

In **Genesis 1:29**, God describes to us what His original diet for man consisted of. It included fruits, grains and nuts. As already mentioned previously (ch.4), vegetables were added later (**Gen. 3:18**) to man's diet after the fall of man. In the Garden of Eden there was a tree of life. This tree is described in **Revelation 22:2-3** as bearing 12 different types of fruit each month and it mentioned that the leaves were for the healing of the nations. It is not the attempt of this book to debate the various theological and medical discussions on the proper diet but only to give credence for a diet that God approved of in the very beginning.

Although not a popular concept, a plant-based diet is a better diet for man. This diet has more phytochemicals, fiber and minerals and less cholesterol and fats than an animal based diet. There is a plethora of studies that verify that a vegetarian diet, which primarily consist of whole grains, fruits, vegetables and nuts (also legumes), helps to prevent and treat chronic diseases.[9] A plant-based diet also contributes to lower blood cholesterol, reduced risk of diabetes, heart disease, stroke and cancer.[10] In a 20 year study completed by Loma Linda University, it was shown that individuals who were on a vegan (free of animals products of any kind) diet lived 15 years longer than meat eaters.[11] Other research sources such as the China Study, Preventive Medicine, Journal of the American Medical Association, American Journal of Public Health and British Medical Journal gives validity to the fact that a plant based diet is the best diet to increase longevity and general well-being.

There have been some skeptics that feel as though a vegetarian diet is lacking in certain vitamins, in particular, vitamin B_{12}. It is true that vitamin B_{12} sources are primarily from the animal kingdom; however, it is not the only source. Contrary to popular belief, B_{12} can actually be found in plant-based sources. Because B_{12} comes from the soil, it has been determined that if the soil is enriched with organic fertilizer, the results are an increased production of vitamin B_{12} which can be absorbed by various plants. Since the required amount for the human body is approximately 2 mcg per day, one could easily get the required amount by eating 3-4 ounces of organic spinach per day.[12] Other natural sources of B_{12} are turnip greens, raw sunflower seeds, concord grapes, raw honey and fruits and vegetables eaten directly from a tree or vine.[13] In order to know for sure whether you are getting enough B_{12} you can take a blood test. I am a vegan and have just recently received a blood test and my levels of B_{12} were very high. I do not take any vitamin B_{12} supplements.

Vegetarianism in and of itself does not necessarily constitute dietary health. There are many unhealthy vegetarians and there are some healthy meat eaters. There are a few basic principles of eating that I believe will help to establish proper nutrition:

> ➢ Eat a balanced diet (***Prov. 23:19-21***)— Eat a variety of raw "live" foods (primarily fruits and vegetables). Be sure to eat plenty of whole grains and nuts (legumes, tofu, kosher meat (refer to Chapter 4), etc.) sparingly. If you eat fish, be aware that they may contain chemicals and toxins (especially mercury that may be harmful to your health). Be very selective and try to choose pesticide free fish.
> ➢ Eat in moderation. Generally speaking, we eat too much! Too much food, too much fat, too much sugar, too much salt and too much dead or dying foods (overcooked). We need

to stop the madness! Think before putting anything in your mouth, read labels carefully and plan the types of foods for consumption that's good for you and that taste good. Educate your taste buds. Don't eat compulsively! Everything that smells and taste good is not always good for human consumption.

➤ Eat (as much as possible) foods free of chemicals, preservatives, additives, artificial flavorings and colorings, trans fat or hydrogenated oils.

➤ Eat real food (an apple) versus artificially based food (apple flavored cereal)) and whole grains versus enriched grains. Limit refined and processed foods. Most of the food items that are in a box, can or package are full of chemicals, preservatives and enhanced flavorings. Choose your food intelligently.

Perhaps it would benefit us to take the ten day challenge that Daniel and his friends took in the first chapter of book Daniel. They refused to eat the rich foods and the wine appointed by the king of Babylon. They instead challenged the chief of the eunuchs to give them vegetables and water to drink. After ten days of consuming this type of diet, Daniel and his friends were 10 times healthier physically, intellectually and spiritually. Just like God blessed Daniel and friends and restored Job double-fold of all he loss, He is anxious to restore us in every area of our lives if we would follow Heaven's wellness system.

Chapter XI

The Faith Factor

> **Hebrews 11:1, (Amplified) —**
> *NOW FAITH is the assurance (the confirmation, the title deed) of the things [we] hope for, being the proof of things [we] do not see and the conviction of their reality [faith perceiving as real fact what is not revealed to the senses].*

If you were diagnosed with a grave disease or illness, who would be the very first person that you would turn to for help—your husband or wife, your mother or father, your doctor or your natural remedies? Most of us would turn to our doctor. Why? Because we are programmed to look to the doctor for every thing that ails us. Generally, this means the taking of pills, drugs or having surgery done to improve our condition. The problem I have with this is that most of the time, God is left out of the picture. God the Author of life is generally the last person who we turn to when faced with an illness or disease that may lead to death. Even though there may be some doctors who acknowledge God as the real Healer, the majority of them do not view God as a viable part of the healing process. As Christians and believers in the Creator God—how is it that we have so little faith and trust in the God who created us and who knows more about the human machinery than anyone? God was very disappointed with King Asa *(2 Chron. 16:11-13)* when he turned to the physicians instead of Him. Perhaps had he turned to God for healing, the scenario could have been reversed.

I believe the issue boils down to a doctor who we can see versus a God who we cannot visibly see. Doesn't it seem strange that we are to believe in a God whom we cannot see with the naked eye? Yet that is exactly what God wants us to do *(2 Cor. 5:7)*. Since it is God's desire for us the exercise this type of faith, the most logically question to ask is, "How do we develop or possess such a faith? The first step is to look at the evidence. Just for the sake of comparison, let's take a glimpse of the results of trusting in the physician (man) versus Physician (God) in the treatment of most illnesses:

Physician (man)	Physician (God)
1. Treats the symptoms	1. Cures the cause
2. Adjusts the body's metabolism in an attempt to stimulate healing through drugs, pills, and surgery.[1]	2. Balances the body system through diet, water, exercise, rest, herbs, and other natural remedies.
3. Temporary	3. Permanent
4. Side effects	4. No side effects
5. Kills good and bad bacteria	5. Produces life giving properties
6. Breaks down the immune system	6. Boost the immune system

God's ways are always superior to man's way. God has created man with gifts and talents to be of service to each other and this would include the services of a physician; however, our dependence must not be on man but on God. God has proven Himself to be the Great Physician by providing us with healing properties necessary to combat harmful substances that we eat, breathe in and consume. He gives us vitamin D by way of the sun to strengthen our bones. He supplies us with ample water for drinking, cleansing, detoxing and healing. He even created foods and herbs that in their natural state are complete with life-giving properties (vitamins, minerals, phytochemicals, antioxidants, etc.). He provides us with air that we breathe to sustain life and to oxygenate the blood, clean the bronchial sacs and lungs and help us to sleep soundly. If God find-tuned the atmosphere (**Gen. 2:7**) so that we can breathe, how can we doubt Him! Most importantly though, God has provided us with great and precious promises which we can cling to and find healing for our body, mind, and soul (**Ps. 103:3; Deut. 7:15; Ex. 23:25, 26; Jer. 17:7; 30:17; Ps. 41:2, 3**).

The problem I have with medical doctors is that the majority of them do not collaborate with the Great Physician in utilizing His methods of healing along with their God-given abilities and gifts. Let me just clear up any preconceived ideas about my beliefs regarding the function of medical doctors. Medical professionals are very much needed and play an essential role in the healing of sickness and disease of humankind; however, I do not believe that their function should supersede the wisdom and the healing ways of the Almighty God. To be perfectly honest, when it comes to internally adjusting the intricate working of the human body[2], I believe that a lot of times medicines fail. Traditional medicine today emphasizes the treatment of symptoms but very seldom get to the root of the problem which 80-90% of the time is lifestyle related. God in His infinite wisdom has created our bodies with the capacity to heal and to maintain good health through His marvelous resources and His all powerful ability to heal through His Word.

One of the biggest obstacles that most of us face in our Christian experience is "unbelief." We really don't believe what God says in His Word and we really don't believe that He will do just what He says. I will give a personal illustration to bring clarity to these points:

While I was getting treatment for follicular lymphoma which included a heat treatment (hydrotherapy),[3] a treatment where you are in a tub full of hot water for a time in order raise your temperature up to a point where the body is warring off cancer cells, I remembered that a furniture company was to deliver our bedroom set between the hours of 11:00 a.m. and 1:00 p.m. I had already started my treatment at approximately 10:00 a.m. The whole treatment process takes about two hours. I began to get a little concerned that they may arrive while I was in the Jacuzzi and I would be unable to answer the door to let them in—so I prayed, "Lord, please make it so that the furniture company will not arrive until around 12 noon or later." Not even 30 minutes had passed (10:30 a.m.) and I became very anxious, still wondering whether or not they would show up before I completed my treatment. So, I began to pray again, "Lord you know I need to complete this treatment; please delay their coming until 12 noon or later." As I continued to become more and more anxious, I hear God speak to me through His Spirit and said, "Didn't you just pray to Me about this situation?" I replied, "Yes I did." God said, "so why are you anxious and worried; don't you believe in the prayers that you have prayed to me, or do you even believe that I will do what you have asked of me?" Then God spoke in my Spirit something that really shook me up. He said, "If you can't trust me with the little things then how do you expect to be healed if you do not believe?" It then dawned on me that I was praying with a heart of disbelief. I asked myself, "If you don't believe God is going to answer your prayer, why are you praying?" I was convicted and I immediately prayed, "Lord please forgive my unbelief; I believe that You can do anything and I am leaving this situation in Your capable hands. I instantly felt peace, no longer worried or anxious. I relaxed and enjoyed my whirlpool bath, although it was quite hot. Whether the company came early or late, I believed that God would work everything out. God in His infinite mercy and love, rewarded my meager faith and the furniture company did not arrive until around 12:45 p.m. I was able to usher them in "fully clothed and in my right mind."

I am reminded of what Jesus said in **Mark 11:22-24 (Amplified)**, *"Have faith in God [constantly]. Truly I tell you, whoever says to this mountain, Be lifted up and thrown into the sea! and does not doubt at all in his heart but believes that what he says will take place, it will be done for him. For this reason I am telling you, whatever you ask for in prayer, believe (trust and be confident) that it is granted to you, and you will [get it]."* Let's pray and ask God to help us remove the obstacle (mountain) of unbelief and cast it in the sea and believe and not doubt so that we will receive.

How to Experience Faith in God

As I pondered on this topic of how the faith factor relates to the healthy anointed life I could not but notice that it is indeed the most important contributing factor. We cannot live the healthy anointed life without faith in the God that provides the anointing. So I am in agreement with the writer who states that, Faith in God contributes far more to positive health than the most powerful medicine (traditional or alternative).[4] I'd like to suggest to you six points that will help you experience greater faith in God:

1. Develop a personal relationship with God by spending quality time with Him each day.

The Bible says that faith comes by hearing and hearing from the Word of God. In order to have faith we must take the time out to hear from Him. I would dare say....more than 10 minutes a day (refer to the time chart Chapter 9).

2. Ask God for more faith. God has promised to give all who ask a measure of faith

3. Act upon that measure of faith God has given you. Any worthwhile gift must be exercised in order to develop and grow that gift.

4. Cooperate with the promptings of the Holy Spirit. Be obedient to what God is asking you to do at every given moment.

5. Wait with expectancy and total trust. I believe the ingredients for faith include peace (rest), assurance (belief), hope (expectancy), patience (waiting) and obedience (submission).

As wonderful as faith is, we must not put our faith in our ability to have faith (putting faith in faith) but rather put our faith in God. It is God who heals not faith. **Psalm 62:5** says *"My soul, wait silently for God alone, for my expectation is from Him."*

Chapter XII

A Higher Calling

> **Colossians 3:1** — *So if you're serious about living this new resurrection life with Christ, act like it. Pursue the things over which Christ presides. Don't shuffle along, eyes to the ground, absorbed with the things right in front of you. Look up, and be alert to what is going on around Christ—that's where the action is. See things from his perspective.*
> **(Message)**

God is calling us to higher aspirations, a higher purpose, and higher expectations in each area of *"the healthy anointed life."* It is time to stop patterning our holistic health conceptions on the world's philosophy and principles. We must look to Jesus for health, healing and restoration. Our concepts of health, physically, mentally, and spiritually must be based on the Word of God. As Christians, we are buying into everything that the world says is good for us. Concepts of fashion (dress), social outlets (entertainment), proper foods (diet), healing methods (traditional or alternative), and spirituality (truth) must be based on a "thus says the Lord" and not necessarily from secular avenues.

Who said it is okay to listen, watch or participate in all kinds of provocative (sexual), perverse (cursing, alternative lifestyle, etc), and violent (crimes) scenarios depicted on the screen at the movie theater, at home on TV, on DVDs, or the computer? Who said it is okay to eat any and everything from most fast food restaurants that serve foods that are loaded with fat (heart disease), salt (hypertension) and sugar (diabetes)? Who said it is okay to take pills, drugs, and chemotherapy to cure all forms of illnesses and all forms of cancer? Who said it was okay to adopt the style of dress in which pants sag below the rear end in order to show an array of colorful briefs, not to mention cleavage exposure, tightly-fitting jeans, skirts, and dresses that are so short that when they sit everything is revealed? It's bad enough to see our society buy into this type of lifestyle, but it is even worst to see "born-again Christians" conduct and model their lifestyle after the world.

We must move up to a higher standard, a higher vision, and a higher calling. We must educate ourselves not only by every Word that proceeds out of mouth of God but also by paying attention to research and literature so that we are aware of fads, gimmicks, propaganda and certainly, reality. Did you know that obesity in the United States has risen to an all time high of 40%

in some populations primarily because of what we eat?[1] Are you aware that the leading cause of death is contributed to conventional medicine (adverse drug reaction, medical errors, etc.).[2] Are you cognizant of the fact that high levels of free radicals in the body, which is the fundamental cause of most diseases, are contributed to environmental pollutants, alcohol, smoking, and unhealthy foods (fats, refined and processed foods).[3] Have you been informed that every conceivable type of heinous crime is conjured up in the mind basically by what we watch, hear and dwell on?[4]

It all boils down to who and what are we looking to for knowledge, wisdom, and understanding as to how to live the healthy anointed life. We need to be renewed, enlightened, and heightened to reach the exalted attainments that God would have us to reach. A life that is altogether new—new body, new mind, new spirit, new affections, new interests, new thoughts, new job and, possibly, new friends. We must withdraw from the companionship with Satan and worldly pursuits and yoke up with Jesus and soar the heights of godliness, righteousness, and holiness.

In **Proverbs 29:18**, the Bible says "*Where there is no vision, the people perish: but he that keepeth the law, happy is he.*" I am reminded that in this text the word "vision" is actually talking about a Word from God. Without applying the Word of God in our lives, we perish. What is your vision? Is it to prosper in your body, mind, and spirit? That is exactly what God has in store for you (**3 Jn. 2**). You are not alone in your quest for prosperity! It is God's desire to prosper you in every dimension of your life. He is birthing dreams of prosperity in you. He said that *"He is able to do exceedingly abundantly above all that we can ask or think (**Eph. 3:20**)."* Do you believe Him? **(Pause and Reflect.)**

What are your aspirations today? God can fulfill them. A renewed mind? God can restore it! A healthy body? God can heal it! A close and more intimate relationship with God? God has ordained it! A financial breakthrough? God can supply it! A godly life-partner? God can find him or her for you! Whatever it is, God can perform it, provide it or produce it!

Jesus came to this earth for the purpose of restoring us back to the image of our Maker in every aspect of our life. Will you accept this amazing anointing and transformation today? Then go ahead; walk in your healing in every area of your life!

Chapter XIII

Holistic Health Restored (Personal Testimony)

> *Psalm 103: 1-4 — Bless the LORD, O my soul; And all that is within me, bless His holy name! Bless the LORD, O my soul, And forget not all His benefits, Who forgives all your iniquities, Who heals all your diseases, Who redeems your life from destruction, Who crowns you with lovingkindness and tender mercies,*

It is my intention throughout this personal testimony to bless (glorify, testify, praise, and magnify) the living God, with all my being, for all of His marvelous acts and His life-sustaining gifts, because He deserves nothing less from me than to use of all my faculties to praise and glorify His name! Verse two of **Psalm 103** admonishes us not to forget all of His benefits. A renowned author once wrote that we have nothing to fear for the future unless we forget how God has led us in the past. When you are going through a crisis, it is so easy to forget how God had delivered or led you through one trial after another in the past. But this text tells us not to forget. What are these benefits that we are not to forget? They are that God forgives us of every one of our sins and heals us of all of our diseases. Hallelujah! Glory be to God! Notice the adjective "all" used to describe how many of our sins are forgiven and what types of diseases are healed. **ALL!** The benefits continue; God saves our lives from death and hell and heaps on our head a crown of love, kindness, and mercy. Thank you Jesus! These promises are a source of comfort and hope to me and can be to anyone who will believe and receive.

It was the year of 2008, and life was abundant with blessings. I had finally finished my Ph.D. (2007), I had been promoted to full Professor, and I had just gotten married to a wonderful, God-fearing man. I was serving as the Chair in the Department of Health, Wellness and Physical Education at Columbia Union College near D.C. My children were grown; one is married and the other one was beginning her graduate studies. This was the time to settle down with my husband and begin to really enjoy life without the responsibilities of parenting (young children). You see, I had been a single parent for almost 20 years basically without the support of others. I had finally gotten to a point where I could begin to do things for myself that I was unable to do while supporting two children through Christian schools and supplying their various needs.

My plan backfired when on July 25, 2008, I was diagnosed with follicular lymphoma—a cancer of the lymph nodes that is said to be incurable. My oncologist shared with me that the only thing he could do was to perform chemotherapy in an effort to prolong my life. He also shared with me that, because of how widely the lymphoma had spread, if I didn't take chemo or radiation treatments I would probably die within a year or so. Needless to say, this was devastating news, especially in light of the fact that I had lived a healthy lifestyle for the past 30 years. As I mentioned previously, I wept bitterly—you know, that kind of weeping that just swells from the pit of your stomach, and I questioned God's rationale. *Why God? Why would you allow me to experience this grave illness, especially when I had tried to live a healthy lifestyle?* I cried and prayed, and prayed and cried.

Because God reigns and rules in my life, I petitioned Him for guidance. Should I take the chemo as the doctor suggested or go an alternative route? I decided, by the prompting of the Holy Spirit, to fast and pray about this situation. I called a dear friend of mine (Shirley) who is a woman of faith and a prayer warrior, to intercede and pray with me. We decided to pray and fast for ten days, asking the Lord for insight on how I should proceed. At the end of fasting and praying for ten days, the Lord impressed upon both of us that His will for me was that I trust in Him for healing and follow various natural means of restoration. Now, in her prayer, my spiritual partner asked the Lord for confirmation regarding the decision that we felt the Lord was leading me to incorporate. That same day, my youngest daughter called to ask me what type of treatment I was going to do. I hesitated because, initially, she was not in favor of me using natural treatments; however, I proceeded to tell her that I felt the Lord was prompting me to treat the disease naturally. To my surprise, she said, "Mom, I totally support you in this." I began to cry because God in His infinite wisdom gave my friend and I the confirmation that we prayed for.

About a month or so after that decision, my husband and I ventured out to Seale, Alabama (Uchee Pines Lifestyle Center) to learn about God's natural ways to heal. We stayed at the Lifestyle Center for approximately three weeks and then headed home with a new lifestyle regimen and renewed hope in a positive outcome of healing.

The adjustments with the new lifestyle changes were challenging and I was not able to keep up with all of the various treatments that I received at the Lifestyle Center. It was at this point that I began a faith journey with God that has completely changed my life. I had become very stressed and frustrated because I wasn't able to keep up with the program which consisted of hydrotherapy, charcoal poultices, juicing, green smoothies, preparing special foods (80% raw, 20% cooked), herb teas, drinking lots of water, exercise, 8-9 hours of rest every night, and spending time in devotion and prayer. I began agonizing with Lord to help me to be faithful on the regimen so that I could get better. You see, at this point, my focus was on the healing methods and not on the Healer.

It wasn't until I went back to the oncologist and received some very disappointing news that the cancer had grown that I began to change my focus to the Healer and not the healing methods. Please don't misunderstand me; I truly believe that God works through His natural healing methods, but it is God who heals!

My emphasis was now focused on a complete dependence on the only One who could restore my health. Although I did the best that I could do on my lifestyle program, I was no longer stressed if I didn't get everything in because my dependence was on the Words (promises) of God. I took a package of index cards and wrote out every text that I could find that dealt with healing and restoration. I began to realize that it was actually God's desire to heal me, and although God wants me to follow sound health principles, it is His power that heals, not my works.

The disease continued to progress, but my focus continued to be on the promises of God. I shared with you that one my most discouraging moments was when I began to experience a host of swollen lymph nodes that were pressing against my neck, my throat, and my ear lobes. They were under my armpits, and in the groin areas. They were literally popping up all over. The enemy whispered in my ear, "You are going to die." I cried out to the Lord and said, "If you don't do something soon, I'm not going to make it." The Lord put this promise on my heart—"If you diligently heed the voice of the LORD your God and do what is right in His sight, give ear to His commandments and keep all His statutes, I will put none of the diseases on you which I have brought on the Egyptians. For I *am* the LORD who heals you." He then added; *"It doesn't matter if you have a hundred swollen lymph nodes, I* **AM** *the Lord who heals you."*

Months had passed and God was teaching me new insights on faith, trust, and total reliance on Him. I stopped looking and feeling for swollen lymph nodes and continued to walk by faith and not in what I can see, touch, or feel. God's Word was (and continues to be) my reality. Some of the promises that have sustained me are: **Proverbs 3:5-8, Psalm 33:18, 19; 30:2-3, Jeremiah 30:17, Exodus 23:25, 26, 2 Corinthians10: 4-6, Psalm 91:14-16** and many more.

A year or so after my unfavorable diagnosis, God has shown me that He is a God that keeps His promises. All of my lymph nodes had decreased in size and most of them have completely disappeared. Praise and honor to the Almighty God! My faith has grown and the sense of God's presence in my life is all-consuming. God says to me, and all who come to Him, "I love you with and everlasting love—a love that never ends—a love that is constant—a love that is reassuring—a love that will never leave you nor forsake you." Glory be to God!

I would like to share two lessons of many that I have learned throughout this faith journey:

> ➤ **It is God's desire to save every one us from all of our sins**

"For God so loved the world that He gave His only begotten Son, that whoever believes in

Him should not perish but have everlasting life" (**Jn. 3:16**).

"That if you confess with your mouth the Lord Jesus and believe in your heart that God has raised Him from the dead, you will be saved. For with the heart one believes unto righteousness, and with the mouth confession is made unto salvation" (**Rom. 10:9-10**).

"For "*whoever calls on the name of the Lord shall be saved*" (**Rom. 10:13**).

"Who desires all men to be saved and to come to the knowledge of the truth" (**1 Tim. 2:4**).

God has ordained us to be saved from the foundation of the world. Salvation is our calling and election given to us through Christ Jesus. Although it is God's will to save us, not all will be saved. Why? Because some of us are not willing to allow Jesus to save us or to do what is necessary to be saved (we are instructed to accept Christ as Savior and Lord in your life; make Christ's way of life our way of life; establish a relationship with God, obey and cooperate with the promptings of the Holy Spirit). Most of the time, it is our choices that keep us from fulfilling God's will to save us. Nevertheless, it is still God's heartfelt desire that all be saved.

> **It is also God's desire to heal every one of us from all of our diseases**

"Beloved, I pray that you may prosper in all things and be in health, just as your soul prospers" (*3 Jn. 2*).

"For I will restore health to you And heal you of your wounds,' says the LORD" (*Jer. 30:17*).

"And the prayer of faith will save him who is sick, and the Lord will restore him; and if he has committed sins, he will be forgiven" (*Jas. 5:15, Amplified*)

"When evening had come, they brought to Him many who were demon-possessed. And He cast out the spirits with a word, and healed all who were sick, that it might be fulfilled which was spoken by Isaiah the prophet, saying, *"He Himself took our infirmities And bore our sicknesses"* (*Matt. 8:16, 17*).

God has decreed our healing from the foundation of the world when He decided to sacrifice His Son Jesus Christ for our sins.
Even though God desires to heal us, not all will be healed. Why? Because some of us either do not truly believe that God can heal us or are not willing to do what God tells us to do in order to be healed (again, we are required to accept Christ as Savior and Lord in our lives; make Christ's way

of life our way of life; believe, have confidence in and claim His promises; establish a close relationship with God by spending quality time with Him; and obey His health principles {lifestyle change}).

Too many of us want to be saved and healed by our own design and our own way, but not necessarily God's way. If we want to be completely restored, we must be willing to cooperate with the Spirit. God works with each individual differently and He is able to save and heal to the utmost. He chose to heal me through His natural healing resources. I believe that is the way He prefers; however, God can heal anyway He wants to. Our job is to listen to His Voice and follow His Way.

I want to point out that God does not always change the consequences of the choices that we or our parents make, otherwise we would not be free agents of choice; nevertheless, I believe it is still His desire to save us and to heal us. God knows the end from the beginning and He also knows our hearts, thoughts, motives, and our future circumstances. Everything is open to His all-seeing eye. So, we can be confident that He will act according to His divine purpose in our lives.

I would like to end my testimony with a revised quote from an inspired writer, "God is just as willing to restore the sick to health now as when the Holy Spirit spoke those words to the Psalmist (3 John 2), and Christ is the same compassionate physician now that He was during His earthly ministry. In Him there is a healing balm for every disease [that includes the physical, mental, spiritual, emotional, social and occupational ailments] and restoring power for every infirmity." By His Stripes we have been healed!

In the pages that follow, I have included recipes that I have used, and continue to use. While they are not intended to be medicinal, or curative, they are being shared in response to a number of requests that I have received. I trust that you would enjoy them as I do.

Appendix A

Almost All Raw Recipes

Most of the raw recipes require a sturdy blender and a good quality food processor. A few raw recipes might also require a dehydrator.

There are quite a few raw recipes that are in various books, on the internet and those that can be easily created by experimenting with different combinations of raw foods. The following recipes are favorites of mine and they are from different resources. A few ingredients may have been added or deleted but I cannot claim them as my own. There are some that are specifically named after the original creator of the recipe while others are not labeled as such:

Almond Milk

1 cup almonds (soaked for at least 24 hours)*
2 cups water
1 tablespoon agave nectar or raw honey
1 teaspoon vanilla extract
1/2 teaspoon sea salt

Place ingredients in blender and mix thoroughly. Strain through cheese cloth and squeeze out all liquid. You can freeze the almond pulp for another use.

Banana Milk

1 frozen banana
1 cup water
1 teaspoon flaxseed oil
1 teaspoon vanilla extract
1/4 teaspoon sea salt

Place ingredients in blender and mix thoroughly. You may use it over cereal (granola, oatmeal, etc.) or drink as a glass of milk.

Green Smoothie

2 cups of greens (any combination – i.e. spinach, romaine, kale)
1/4 cup of cilantro
1 tablespoon of barley green powder
1 teaspoon of spirulina
1 teaspoon of chlorella
1 apple (cored)
1 banana (fresh or frozen)
6 oz organic apple or pineapple juice

Place all ingredients in blender. Blend until smooth and creamy. For a different flavor, you may use other types of fruit in place of the ones listed. This is one of the healthiest drinks that you can consume. It is full of healing properties and gives you increased energy.

Grits

1/4 head of cauliflower (caps only)
1/2 avocado
1 teaspoon onion powder
1/8 teaspoon sea salt

In food processor fitted with 'S' blade, break down the cauliflower until grainy. Next mash the avocado with the onion powder and sea salt and mix in the cauliflower granules and enjoy.

Raw Blueberry Pancakes

3 cups oat groats (soaked for 24 hours)
1/3 cup of almonds (soaked for 24 hours)
3 tablespoon agave nectar or raw honey
1 apple
1 cup blueberries
1 teaspoon vanilla extract
1/4 sea salt
A pinch of cinnamon (optional)

Blend all ingredients in food processor until smooth. Scoop onto the dehydrator trays (covered with parchment paper). Dehydrate for 8-10 hours at 105° F. Top with pine nut sauce.

Pine Nut Sauce

1/2 cup soaked pine nuts
1/2 cup filtered water
3 tablespoon pure maple syrup
1 teaspoon vanilla flavoring
A pinch of sea salt

Blend all ingredients in blender until smooth and creamy. Great over pancakes or over fruit.

*Soaked (germinated) nuts, seeds, and grains increases the production of enzymes, minerals, vitamins, and amino acids 200% or more. They are also more easily digestible. (Dr. Edward Howard, *Enzyme Nutrition*)

Raw Oatmeal
11/2 cup oat groats (soaked)
1/4 cup almonds (soaked)
1 banana
1 apple
1/2 cup strawberries
1/4 cup dates (washed and soaked until soft)
1/4 teaspoon vanilla flavor
1/8 teaspoon sea salt
A pinch of cinnamon (optional)

Blend well in a food processor. Should look similar to cooked oatmeal, only more healthy and taste better. Enjoy! Try it warm using a dehydrator with almond milk.

*Claire's Mashed Potatoes
2 cups cashews
2 cups almond milk
1 avocado
1 cauliflower
1/4 onion
1 teaspoon olive oil
1/4 teaspoon sea salt
1/2 teaspoon tahini

Place all ingredients in a food processor with "S" blade attachment and blend everything together until smooth.

Mushroom Gravy

2 cups crimini mushrooms
2 Tablespoons Bragg Liquid Aminos
1 Tablespoon water
1 small garlic clove
1/2 teaspoon sage
1/4 teaspoon sea salt

Place in food processor and blend until smooth. Pour over mashed potatoes.

Pimento Cheese

1/2 cup pine nuts
1/2 cup macadamia nuts
1/2 cup sunflower seeds
1 small to medium red bell pepper
1/2 lemon peeled
2 cloves garlic
2 Tablespoon Bragg Liquid Aminos (add more or less, depending on how sharp you like it)

Place nuts in food processor and grind into fine powder, then add the remaining ingredients and blend until smooth. You may also use raw cashews in place of the nuts and seeds.

*Claire Benson is a good friend of mine and a fabulous cook. She is an innovative vegetarian, vegan and raw-vegan chef.

Apple Sauce
4 apples (your choice)
1 tablespoons agave nectar
1/2 teaspoon cinnamon
1/4 teaspoon vanilla

Dice apples into chunks (your choice if you wish to peel the apples or not). Place all ingredients into your food processor and blend until smooth.

Guacamole
2 avocados
1/4 cup onion
1 small tomato
1/4 teaspoon of garlic powder
1/4 teaspoon sea salt
A pinch of cayenne
Cilantro (optional)

Blend all ingredients together.

Mango Salsa
2 mangoes
1 lime, juiced
1 garlic clove
1/2 bunch of chopped fresh cilantro (optional)
1 teaspoon of raw agave nectar
1 teaspoon green chili pepper

Blend all ingredients in a food processor except one mango. Place mixture into a bowl, dice remaining mango into small pieces and add to mixture and stir. Chill and serve. You can make a pineapple mango salsa by adding pineapple to this recipe.

Hummus

4 cups sprouted chickpeas
1 cup tahini
1 cup onions
1 cup olive oil
1 cup lemon, peeled
1-2 cloves of garlic
1 tablespoon Bragg Liquid Aminos
1/8 teaspoon sea salt

Place all ingredients in food processor and blend until smooth.
Note: you can add different vegetables such as red bell pepper, carrots, etc., and change the flavor according to your likes.

Zucchini Hummus

5 cups zucchini, peeled and chopped
1/2 cup tahini
4 cloves garlic
1/2 cup lemon juice
1/4 cup olive oil
1/2 teaspoon paprika
1/8 teaspoon cayenne and/or cumin
1 1/2 teaspoons sea salt

Place all ingredients in food processor and blend until smooth.

Salsa
4 tomatoes, chopped
2 scallions
2 cloves garlic
1/2 cup parsley
1/2 cup cilantro
1 Tablespoon Bragg Apple Cider Vinegar
1 Tablespoon Olive oil
1 Tablespoon lime juice
1 teaspoon cumin
1 teaspoon sea salt
Jalapeno to taste

Place the lime juice, jalapeno, cilantro, parsley, garlic, cider vinegar, olive oil, cumin and salt in a food processor blend until well ground. Add the scallion and tomatoes and pulse chop until everything is diced and blended.

Refried Beans (1) by Bonzai Aphrodite
Presoak the first two ingredients together for 4 hours
1/4 dried chipotle chili (pepper)
8 sundried tomatoes
2 cups sunflower seed soaked and drained
1/2 jalapeno pepper washed and de-seeded
2 green onions, chopped
1/4 cups cilantro with stems, chopped
1/4 teaspoon chili powder
1/4 teaspoon salt
1/4 teaspoon cumin powder
1/4 cup olive oil
1/4 teaspoon chopped garlic
1 teaspoon lemon juice

Purée the seeds, tomatoes, chipotle into a smooth paste in food processor fitted with "S" blade. Place the rest of the ingredients in the food processor and continue and puree until smooth.

Refried Beans (2)
1 cups sprouted chickpeas
1 cup walnuts
2 avocadoes
4 Tablespoons lime juice
2 teaspoons olive oil
4 teaspoons cumin
1/4 teaspoon cayenne pepper
Sea salt to taste

Place all ingredients in food processor and pulse chop until chunky, and then add the avocado and pulse; chop until desired consistency is achieved.

Potato Salad
2 pounds jicama, cubed small
1 red bell pepper diced
2 ears of corn, scraped off the cob (or fresh frozen corn kernels)
2 stalks celery, diced
1 medium onion, diced
1 avocado, diced
1/2 cup tahini
2 cloves garlic, minced
1/3 cup lemon juice
1 Tablespoon cilantro
1 teaspoon cumin
1/2 teaspoon chili powder
4 teaspoon fresh dill
2 teaspoons sea salt

Mix all ingredients together and pour some of Claire's Raw Mayonnaise recipe over the top if you like, and chill for a few hours before serving.

Claire's Raw Mayonnaise
1/2 cup soaked almonds (blanched)
1 Tablespoon pine nuts
1 Tablespoon agar-agar flakes
1/2 clove garlic
1/2 cup water
1/2 cup olive oil
1/2 cup sunflower oil
1 Tablespoon flax seed oil
8 Tablespoons lemon juice
1 teaspoon Bragg apple cider vinegar
1 teaspoon agave nectar
1/2 teaspoon mustard powder
1/4 teaspoon Celtic sea salt

Blend the first 5 ingredients until smooth, and then slowly add the oil and then the remaining ingredients.

Wild Rice
1/2 Wild rice sprouted
1 avocado mashed
1/2 teaspoon agave nectar (optional)
1 teaspoon onion powder
1/2 teaspoon sea salt

Mash avocado with onion powder sea salt and agave and mix well, then mix in the rice and enjoy.

Wild Rice Salad

2 cups sprouted wild rice
2 red bell peppers, diced
2 carrots, dices
2 zucchini, diced
2 stalks celery, dices
Dressing of your choice, or
1/4 cup agave nectar
1/4 cup white miso
1/4 tablespoon apple cider vinegar
2 tablespoons olive oil

Mix dressing ingredients and pour over rice, mix everything together and let sit for a few hours or overnight.

Italian Dressing

1 cup olive oil
1 cup sweet basil
1 cup fresh parsley
1/2 cup dried Italian seasoning
2 scallions
2 teaspoons onion powder
1 lemon, juiced
2 cloves garlic
1 Tablespoon agave nectar
1/2 teaspoon sea salt

Blend all ingredients in blender and chill for an hour before serving.

Note: The longer this dressing sits the better because all the flavors really marinade together.

Caesar Salad Dressing

1 cup pine nuts
1 Tablespoon flax oil
1 1/2 teaspoon sea salt
1/3 cup olive oil
1 date (pitted and soaked for about 15 minutes)
1 large garlic clove
2 1/2 Tablespoons lemon juice
2 Tablespoons water
1/2 Tablespoon white miso

In your food processor blend the pine nuts, flax oil, and the sea salt until grainy, and pour into bowl. In the same food processor, combine the olive oil, miso, date, garlic, lemon juice, water, and blend. Pour into bowl and mix everything well. If you need more 'bite', then add more lemon juice and salt.

Claire's Hemp Seed Ranch

1/4 cup olive oil
1/2 cup lemon juice
2 tablespoons Nama Shoyu
1 cup water or almond milk
1/2 cup soaked sunflower seeds (presoak for 2 hours)
1 cup hemp seeds
1 teaspoon garlic
1/2 tablespoon chopped jalapeno pepper
1/4 teaspoon salt
1 tablespoon dried or fresh dill
1 Tablespoon onion powder

Blend all these ingredients starting at a low speed and gradually increase it, and then add:

1 sprig of green onion
1/2 cup fresh parsley
1/2 cup fresh cilantro
1/2 yellow bell pepper

Continue blending until all the herbs and well mixed in and the dressing has a good even color. If you like it a little sweeter, add a little agave nectar. Store in the refrigerator.

Mock Blue Cheese
1 cup cashews
1 cup macadamia nuts
1 cup pine nuts
5 Tablespoons lemon juice
2 cloves garlic
3 teaspoons Bragg Liquid Aminos
2 Tablespoons water
1/2 cup olive oil
1/4 cup parsley (flowers only)
3 Tablespoons scallions

Blend everything together until well combined.

Claire's Raspberry Vinaigrette
6 oz (1 small flat) cups raspberries
1/4 cup orange juice
2 Tablespoons olive oil
1/2 Tablespoon lemon juice
1 Tablespoon Bragg Apple Cider Vinegar (Optional)
1 to 2 Tablespoons Agave Nectar (add more if needed)
Sea salt to taste

Blend all ingredients in blender until smooth.

Claire's Rainbow Cole Slaw

2 cups green cabbage shredded in food processor or by hand
2 cups red (purple) cabbage shredded in food processor or by hand
1 cup carrots, shredded
1/4 cup fresh frozen green peas
1/4 cup raisins
1/2 red onion or Vidalia onion diced (optional)
1/8 teaspoon sea salt

Combine all ingredients and toss, then add Claire's raw mayonnaise and enjoy. This is my absolute favorite!

Claire's Marinara Sauce

4 roma tomatoes
12 sundried tomatoes, soaked 1/2 hour
3 dates pitted and soaked 1/2 hour
1/4 cup olive oil
4 cloves garlic
1 sprig sweet basil (leaves only)
2 Tablespoons parsley (flower tops only)
1 Tablespoon Italian seasoning
1/8 teaspoon cayenne pepper (optional)
1 teaspoon sea salt

Place all ingredients into blender and blend well. Keep leftovers in refrigerator. This marinara sauce is better than any cooked sauce I have ever tasted. If you desire, you may add a little raw agave nectar for a sweeter sauce.

Claire's Alfredo Sauce

1 cup macadamia nuts
1 cup almond or brazil nut milk
2 stalks green onions (scallions), chopped
1/2 to 1 small garlic clove
1/2 teaspoon nutmeg
1/2 teaspoon sea salt

Blend until creamy smooth.

Raw Veggie-Chicken Salad

1 1/3 cup oat grouts (soaked for about 12 hours)
1 1/3 cup walnuts (soaked for about 24 hours)
1 1/3 cup almonds (soaked for about 24 hours)
3 stalks celery
1 Vidalia onion or 1/3 red onion
3 Tablespoons Flax Seed Oil
1 Tablespoon agave nectar
3 teaspoons of vegan chicken seasoning
1 to 2 teaspoons sea salt
1/2 teaspoon dill
1/2 lemon, juiced
A dash of cayenne (optional)

Place liquids in food processor first, then add the rest of the ingredients and blend well. You will have to stop your food processor several times to scrape the sides down. Blend until desired consistency is reached. Be sure all excess water is thoroughly drained before blending in food processor.

Claire's Fruit Cobbler

For the Crust:

3 cups pecans (do no soak)
9 dates de-seeded and chopped well, or make "date paste"
1/2 tablespoon cinnamon
1 tablespoon vanilla
1/8 teaspoon salt
In the bowl of your food processor pulse the nuts, cinnamon, salt, and dates then add the vanilla and press into pie plate. Save a little to sprinkle over the top.

For the Filling:

1 sweet apples sliced thinly
1/2 lb strawberries
5 cups sliced thinly
1/4 cup lemon juice
1 tablespoon vanilla
A pinch of salt

Mix the filling ingredients thoroughly and then pour over the crust in the pie plate. Then sprinkle the remaining crust ingredients over the top of the fruit and enjoy.

Claire's Fresh fruit topping
1 cup soaked cashews
1 lb of strawberries
4 to 5 tablespoons agave nectar
1 cup almond milk
1 Tablespoon vanilla
2 Tablespoon lemon juice
A pinch of salt

In a blender, place the liquid ingredients in first then the cashews and puree until smooth. Next, add the strawberries and puree until rich and smooth. Chill and enjoy.

Easy Mock Parmesan Topping
I cup brazil nuts (no need to soak)
1 small garlic clove
Pinch of sea salt

Place in food processor fitted with "S" blade, process till crumb like consistency. Sprinkle over salad, marinara sauce or alfredo sauce.

Red Pepper Aioli
1 cup cashews, soaked for an hour
1/4 cup water
2 garlic cloves, minced
Juice one lemon
1/2 red bell pepper, seeded and chopped
2 tablespoons olive oil
2 teaspoons sea salt

Combine cashews, water, lemon juice and garlic in a blender. Blend until cashew becomes a thick, smooth mayonnaise. Add more water one tablespoon at a time until cashews break down and you achieve desired consistency.

Add in the red peppers, olive oil and sea salt. Briefly process until peppers are smooth. Serve with bread, cucumbers, mushrooms and tomatoes.

Mock Tuna Salad
3 cups walnut, soaked 12 hours
3 cups carrot pieces
1/2 medium onion, chopped in large pieces
1 cup celery pieces
1/2 cup chopped parsley
1/4 cup fresh dill (or 1 tsp dried)
3 cloves garlic
2 lemons, juiced
Dulse flakes

Process the walnuts and carrots first, then add other ingredients to taste. To moisten, mix in the Red Pepper Aioli-recipe (listed above).

Marinated greens
4 heads kale or mixture of favorite greens (this will seem like a lot but will wilt down when the salt is added)
2 tablespoons salt
2 cups baby tomatoes, sliced
1/2 cup diced sweet onions

For dressing:
3 avocados
1-2 crushed garlic
2 chipotle peppers*
1/2 cup olive oil
2 tablespoons agave nectar
1/4 cup lemon juice

*If not using chipotle peppers, substitute with onion powder, cumin, chili powder, garlic powder and tamari/nama shoyu. Remove the stems and then wash and cut the kale into small pieces. Place into small bowl, add salt and start to massage the kale until it wilts and takes on a 'cooked' texture. Add tomatoes to the bowl and mix in by hand. Blend all remaining ingredients in a high-speed blender until creamy and mix into kale by hand.

Appendix B

A Few Cooked Recipes

These recipes are vegan (cooked) recipes, published by demand (smile).

Pizza (raw or slightly cooked)
2 medium-sized (not the small ones) Ezekiel Sprouted Tortillas
1 cup Claire's Marinara Sauce
1 cup pimento cheese
1 cup chopped veggies (onions, black olives, green peppers, etc.)
1 sliced tomato
1 cup grounded up walnuts (seasoned with cumin, coriander and Braggs Liquid Aminos)

Spread the marinara sauce, then the ground walnuts, veggies, slice tomatoes and cheese on the two sprouted tortillas. Warm in oven or dehydrator for 5-10 minutes. Enjoy.

Popcorn (Earlene's original recipe)

1 tablespoon of unrefined extra virgin coconut oil
1/3 cup of unpopped corn
1-2 tablespoon of nutritional yeast
1-2 tablespoon of garlic powder
1 tablespoon of vegan chicken seasoning
Sea salt to taste

Warm up oil in a solid stainless steel pot, add popcorn; be sure not to scorch or burn popcorn. Place popped corn in large bowl, and then add seasonings.

French Toast

Ezekiel Sprouted Raisin Bread
1/4 cup dates
1/2 cup raw cashews
1 cup filtered water
1 teaspoon vanilla flavoring
1/4 teaspoon of sea salt
Cinnamon to taste (optional)
Unrefined extra virgin coconut oil

Place all ingredients, except the bread and oil, in blender. It should be smooth and creamy. Take a small spatula and spread it on top of the bread. Place the bread into a pre-heated skillet with a little coconut oil in it. Cook until brown on one side, than spread the batter on top of the bread, in the skillet, and flip over. Cook until brown. Eat and enjoy! It is great with fruit on top.

German Carob Cake (Adapted from Barbara Watson — The Total Vegetarian)

31/3 cups whole wheat pastry flour
1 tablespoon Rumford Aluminum free baking powder
2 cups of Sucanat or turbinado sugar
1 teaspoon sea salt
6 tablespoons carob powder
1 tablespoon Roma (coffee substitute)
2/3 cup unrefined extra virgin coconut oil (melted)
2 cups water
2 teaspoons vanilla extract

Use two separate bowls; mix the dry ingredients in one and the liquid ingredients in the other. Before combining the ingredients make sure that the oven is pre-heated to 350° and the two 9-inch cake pans are ready (non-stick pans work best). Mix the wet ingredients with the dry ingredients until the majority of the lumps are out. Be sure not to mix the ingredients too long. Put immediately into the cake pans and bake for approximately 30 minutes. Make sure the cake is done by sticking a thin knife in the center of the cake. If it comes out clean it is ready. After it cools, top with coconut walnut frosting.

Coconut Walnut Frosting

2 cups vanilla Silk soy milk
1/2 cup Sucanat
1/2 cup chopped dates
1 teaspoon vanilla extract
1/4 teaspoon sea salt
4 teaspoons cornstarch
2 cups unsweetened, flake coconut
1 cup walnuts, chopped

Place all ingredients except the coconut and walnuts in the blender. It should be creamy and smooth. Pour into a saucepan and cook. Stir continuously over medium heat. When the mixture has thickened, stir in the remaining ingredients. Cool and then spread on both layers of the cake. This cake is absolutely delicious! It is very rich so eat in moderation.

List of Sources

Introduction

1. Ardell, D.B. (1977). High level wellness: An alternative to doctors, drugs, and disease. (2nd Ed.). Berkeley, CA: Ten Speed Press.
2. Hettler, W.H. (1980). Wellness Promotion on a University Campus. *Family and Community Health: The Journal of Health Promotion and Maintenance*, 3, 77-92.
3. Sackney, L., Noonan, B., & Miller, C. M. (2000). Leadership for educator wellness: an exploratory study. *International Journal of Leadership in Education*, 3(1) 41-56.
4. Renger, R. F., Midyett, S. J., Soto, F. G., & Erin, T. D. (2000). Optimal Living Profile: An Inventory to Assess Health and Wellness. *American Journal of Health Behavior*, Vol. 24, Issue 6.
5. Myers, J. E., Sweeney, T. J., and Witmer, J. M. (2000). The Wheel of Wellness Counseling for Wellness: A Holistic

Model for Treatment Planning. *Journal of Counseling & Development*; Vol. 78, 251-266.

6. Brooks, C. W., and Matthews, C. O. (2000). The Relationship among Substance Abuse Counselors' Spiritual Well-being, Values, and Self-Actualizing Characteristics and the Impact on Clients' Spiritual Well-being. *Journal of Addictions Offender Counseling*, 21 (1), 23-31.

7. Pardini, D.A., Plante, T.G., Sherman, A. & Stump, J.E. (2000). Religious faith and spirituality in substance abuse recovery: Determining the mental health benefits. *Journal of Substance Abuse Treatment*, 19, 347-354.

8. Holder et al. (2000). The association between adolescent spirituality and voluntary sexual activity. *Journal of Adolescent Health*, 26, 295-302.

9. Nelson, C. et al. Spirituality, Religion, and Depression in the Terminally Ill. Psychosomatics 43:213-220, June 2002.

10. Myers, J. E., and Williard, K. (2003). Integrating Spirituality Into Counselor Preparation: A Developmental, Wellness Approach. *Counseling and Values*; Vol. 47 (2), 142-155.

11. Ibid.

12. National Wellness Institute (2002). *Holistic Lifestyle Questionnaire*. National Wellness Institute, Inc. http://www.nationalwellness.org. Accessed March 2005.

13. Chockalingam, A. et al. (2004). Estimation of Subjective Stress in Acute Myocardial

Infarction. *Journal of Postgraduate Medicine*; Vol. 50, 3; 207-211.
14. The Wellness Report by Donald B. Ardell (2003). What if the Wellness Concept Were Fully Embraced?
15. Hawks, S. (2004). Spiritual Wellness, Holistic Health, and the Practice of Health Education. *American Journal of Health Education,* 35(1)11-17.
16. NWI (2000).

I - Holistic Healthy Beginnings
1. White, E.G., Story of Redemption (2001). Everlasting Gospel Publishing Association, www.storyofredemption.org.
2. Ibid.
3. Ibid.
4. Ibid.

IV - The Physical Anointed Life
1. U.S. Department of Health and Human Services, *Physical Activity and Health: A Report of the Surgeon General* (CDC, 1999).
2. Journal of the American Medical Association (JAMA), 1999:282 (20) November 24, Morbidity and Mortality Weekly Report/Nutrition.
3. Dean Ornish, et al., *Effects of Stress Management Training and Dietary Changes in Treating Ischemic Heart Disease*, Journal of the Medical Assoc., Vol. 249, no. 1 (1983), pp. 54-59.
4. Michaud DS, Giovannucci E, Willett WC, Colditz GA, Fuchs CS. Dietary meat,

dairy products, fat, and cholesterol and pancreatic cancer risk in a prospective study. Am J Epidemiol. 2003 Jun 15; 157(12):1115-25.

5. Centers for Disease Control and Prevention. *Quick Stats: Percentage of Adults Aged ≥18 Years Who Reported an Average of ≤6 Hours of Sleep per 24-Hour Period, by Sex and Age Group — National Health Interview Survey, United States, 1985 and 2006.* MMWR 2008:57(08); 209.

6. U.S. Census Bureau: The 2010 Statistical Abstract. *Deaths and Death Rates by Leading Causes of Death and Age* (2006).

7. Ibid.

8. *Medicolegal Aspects of Alcohol Determination in Biological Specimens,* which was edited by James C. Garriott and published by PSG Publishing Company, Inc. of Littleton, Massachusetts in 1988.

9. The New Strong's Expanded Dictionary.

10. MayoClinic.com (2009) "Grape Juice: Same Heart Benefits as Wine?"

11. National Institute on Drug Abuse, *"Marijuana: Facts Parents Need to Know"* (2007).

12. Chuder, E.C. (2008) *Neuroscience for Kids Marijuana,* University of Washington.

V - The Intellectual Anointed Life

1. O'Ffill, R. W. (2009) The Fruit of the Spirit: it's what you are that counts. Nampa, Idaho: Pacific Press.

VII - The Emotional Anointed Life
1. The New Strong's Expanded Dictionary.
2. Ibid.

VIII - The Social Anointed Life
1. Webster's New World Dictionary and Thesaurus.
2. Wheeler, M. (2007) *UCLA Researches Identify the Molecular Signature of Loneliness.*
3. Nutt, A. (2007) *Earth Day: 3 R's (Reduce, Reuse and Recycle).* Recycle News and Information.
4. Scott, C. (2007) *Biblical Dating: Just Friends.* www.boundless.org.

IX - The Occupational Anointed Life
1. Burkett, L. (1998) *Money Management for College Students.* Moody, p. 28.
2. US Department of Labor/Bureau of Labor Statistics (2009) *American Time Use Survey.*
3. Nielsenwire (2009) *Americans Watching More TV then Ever: Web and Mobile Up too.*
4. www.youtube.com; *How do you spend your time?*

X - Heaven's Wellness System
1. Thrash, A. (2008) *Exercise.* Uchee Pines Lifestyle Center. Seale, AL.
2. Lite. J. (2009) *Vitamin D deficiency soars in the U.S., study says new research suggests that most Americans are lacking a crucial vitamin,* Scientific American.

3. Thrash, A. (2008) *Sunshine.* Uchee Pines Lifestyle Center. Seale, AL.
4. Schlumpf, Margaret et al. (2001) *In vitro and in vivo estrogenicity of UV screens,* Environmental Health Perspectives, Vol. 109 (239-244).
5. Mann, Denise (2002) *Negative Ions Create Positive Vibes.* WebMD.
6. Lucado, Maxx (2003) *The Great House of God.*
7. Post, S. and Neimark, J. (2007) *Why Good Things Happen to Good People.*
8. Luks, Allan (1991). *The Healing Power of Doing Good: The Health and Spiritual Benefits of Helping Others.*
9. Messina, V. and Burke, K. (1997) *Position of the American Dietetic Association: Vegetarian Diets.* J Am Diet Assoc; 97:1317-21.
10. Craig, W.J. (1999) *Nutrition and Wellness: A Vegetarian Way to Better Health.*
11. Dworkin, N. (1999) *22 Reasons to Go Vegetarians Right Now-benefits of vegetarian diet.* Vegetarian Times.
12. New Century Nutrition (1996) B_{12}: *When Myth Meets Discovery.*
13. Natural Lifestyle and Your Health (1995). *Nutrition and Vitamin B_{12} (cobalamin).*

XI - The Faith Factor

1. Lagerquist, R. (2003) *The North American Diet: Knowledge is Power.* International Bible Society (Book 4 in the Steps to Freedom Series).
2. Ibid.

3. Thrash, A.M. (1981) *Home Remedies: Hydrotherapy, Massage, Charcoal, and Other Simple Treatments.* New Lifestyle Publishing.
4. Solis, D. (2010) Bible Study Guide: Faith and Healing. www.ssnet.com.

XII – A Higher Calling

1. USA Today (2003), *Obesity Predicted for 40% of America.* A better Life, Health education & science.
2. Null, G. et al (2006), *Death by Medicine.*
3. Mayo Clinic (2009), Food Sources the Best Choice for Antioxidants. Donald Hensrud, MD.
4. New Scientist (2007), TV and Film Violence Reaches a New High in 2006. www.cyber-college.com/violence.htm.